ISBN 978-1-330-82310-1
PIBN 10110051

For support please visit www.forgottenbooks.com

1 MONTH OF
FREE
READING

at

www.ForgottenBooks.com

By purchasing this book you are eligible for one month membership to ForgottenBooks.com, giving you unlimited access to our entire collection of over 700,000 titles via our web site and mobile apps.

To claim your free month visit:

www.forgottenbooks.com/free110051

ELEMENTS

OF

LATIN PRONUNCIATION,

FOR THE

USE OF STUDENTS

IN

LANGUAGE, LAW, MEDICINE, ZOOLOGY, BOTANY,
AND THE SCIENCES GENERALLY IN WHICH
LATIN WORDS ARE USED.

BY S. S. HALDEMAN, A. M.,

PROFESSOR OF NATURAL HISTORY IN THE UNIVERSITY OF PENNSYLVANIA.

PHILADELPHIA:
LIPPINCOTT, GRAMBO AND CO.,
SUCCESSORS TO GRIGG, ELLIOT & CO.
1851.

PHILADELPHIA :
T. K. AND P. G. COLLINS, PRINTERS.

PRELIMINARY REMARKS.

HIC ENIM USUS EST LITERARUM, UT CUSTODIANT VOCES ET
VELUT DEPOSITUM REDDANT LEGENTIBUS: ITAQUE ID EXPRI-
MERE DEBENT, QUOD DICTURI SUMUS.—QUINCT. INST. OR. I. VII.

The use of letters is to preserve vocal sounds, and, as it were, return the
deposit to the reader: therefore they should express what we have to say.

In making some inquiries into the phonetic peculiarities of the
aboriginal languages of North America, I found myself at a loss,
from the want of an alphabet in which to record my results, those
of Europe being more or less corrupt; and finding the statements
respecting the Latin alphabet to a certain extent contradictory and
unsatisfactory, I resolved to investigate it, with the intention of
using it strictly according to its Latin signification, as far as this
could be ascertained. This special inquiry being made, a view of
the results is here presented.

Pronunciation is the basis of philology, and without a knowledge of it, in examining the various writings likely to be used for
philological purposes, little progress can be made in this science.
It is of little use to show a person unacquainted with Arabic and
Greek characters, that *kimistry* is derived from كيميا and not
from χυω; or to inform a pupil that the South English word *plow*,
is derived from a North English word, written [plough] with six
characters, if he does not know what words these characters are
intended to represent.

If the learner has better success in Latin words, it may arise
from an acquaintance with many of the characters, as P, F, B, D,
L, T, if they happen to be used in writing his vernacular; but he

of pronunciation; probably not one of whom was consulted by John Walker.*

My results usually agree with those of my predecessors, and when they do not, the adverse opinions are given, so that the reader may exercise his own judment upon them. Deceived by the title, I have procured several English works upon Latin or Greek "pronunciation," which) not contain a word upon the subject. Among the new view will be found the table of the alphabet, (§ 35, note 36a)—an xplanation of the Greek *phi* as the cognate of the digamma al Spanish B—the double nature of H in certain positions—the)wer of the vowel character proposed by Claudius—an additical argument (§ 224, note 58), enforcing Quintilian's view of ie Greek Zeta—a refutation of the English J (§ 230)—the dedstions generally from the natural relations of the elements, and com comparative philology; and many of the illustrations, both atin and transmontane.

The alphabet of no modern nguage corresponds exactly with that of the Latin; although the) is a greater or less resemblance, where there has been an endear to preserve the characters with the powers they have always id, and should always retain in every language using the Rom: alphabet.

Latin is often read as if the ljographs were Italian or German, and with some show of reasoi because the German and Latin letters generally agree, and th full open vowels of the Italian have doubtless been transmitte pure, whilst the elision of syllables in Latin poetry has its cinterpart in Italian versification. ʻee the first note.) In the lipthongs and nasal vowels, the ʻnities are greatest between itin and Portuguese.

Γo what extent that can beconsidered Latin, which a Roman ld not be able to comprehel, can be judged from the so-called ch reading of a German, iho would pronounce the French ʻ written [*poche*] like the ery dissimilar German word spelt ʻ]. This certainly wouldhot be French. An Italian would

*raitsir has published a uful little work on the "Significance of bet;" but it was found pre difficult to get it from Boston, U. S., olumes of Lipsius, Cellcus, and Manutius from Europe.

may be deceived if he fancies that similar characters must indicate similar words, as in the case of the Latin words MARE, MILES, and the English ones *mare, miles.*

The materials upon which this work is founded, are as follows:

1. The ancient grammarians and their
2. Modern commentators.
3. Ancient false orthography.
4. Natural relation of the elements.
5. Interchange of the elements.
6. Ancient words transmitted pure.
7. Names of places transmitted pure.
8. Oriental etymologies.
9. Keltic etymologies.

10. The powers of the alphabet among those nations who adapted their spelling to the successive changes of their language.

A comparison of such materials ought to produce trustworthy results, because, an error which might arise under an individual head, will be likely to be exposed under some of the others. Of these sources, not more than half are usually consulted by writers on the subject.

Under the second head, Schneider's Elements of the Latin Language (Elementarlehre der lateinischen Sprache, Berlin, 1819) is the most valuable, four-hundred pages being devoted to pronunciation, a subject to which about a page is often given, which prevents it from being acquired, except from such professors of the language as have studied it. Dr. Rapp devotes 56 pages to this subject, in his Versuch einer Physiologie der Sprache, Stuttgart, 1836. This work is useful upon the interchange of the vowels; and upon the nasal vowels. Justus Lipsius discusses the subject pretty fully, in his work DE RECTA PRONVNCIATIONE LATINÆ LINGVÆ, ANTVERPLÆ, 1586.

The chief ancient authors to be consulted upon Latin pronunciation are Cicero, Quinctilianus, Marius Victorinus, Terentianus Maurus, Terentius Scaurus, Velius Longus, Priscianus, and Donatus. Schneider quotes fifty ancient authors, upon various points of pronunciation; probably not one of whom was consulted by John Walker.*

My results usually agree with those of my predecessors, and when they do not, the adverse opinions are given, so that the reader may exercise his own judgment upon them. Deceived by the title, I have procured several English works upon Latin or Greek "pronunciation," which do not contain a word upon the subject. Among the new views, will be found the table of the alphabet, (§ 35, note 36a)—an explanation of the Greek *phi* as the cognate of the digamma and Spanish B—the double nature of H in certain positions—the power of the vowel character proposed by Claudius—an additional argument (§ 224, note 58), enforcing Quintilian's view of the Greek Zeta—a refutation of the English J (§ 230)—the deductions generally from the natural relations of the elements, and from comparative philology; and many of the illustrations, both Latin and transmontane.

The alphabet of no modern language corresponds exactly with that of the Latin; although there is a greater or less resemblance, where there has been an endeavor to preserve the characters with the powers they have always had, and should always retain in every language using the Roman alphabet.

Latin is often read as if the logographs were Italian or German, and with some show of reason, because the German and Latin letters generally agree, and the full open vowels of the Italian have doubtless been transmitted pure, whilst the elision of syllables in Latin poetry has its counterpart in Italian versification. (See the first note.) In the dipthongs and nasal vowels, the affinities are greatest between Latin and Portuguese.

To what extent that can be considered Latin, which a Roman would not be able to comprehend, can be judged from the so-called French reading of a German, who would pronounce the French word written [*poche*] like the very dissimilar German word spelt [*poche*]. This certainly would not be French. An Italian would

---

* C. Kraitsir has published a useful little work on the "Significance of the Alphabet;" but it was found more difficult to get it from Boston, U. S., than the volumes of Lipsius, Cellarius, and Manutius from Europe.

be equally in fault, in pronouncing the French words *qui est* differently from his own *chi e.*

An English boy might be inclined to smile at the Latin name SCIPIO, because he fancies that it should agree with his dog's name *Sipio;* but the discrepancy is not due to the Latin, but to a defective education, which leads him to write the English name *Sipio,* with the Roman cay, although he rejects it when writing slave and slander.

Another difficulty arises from a queer association of ideas with what seem to be familiar words, as in the Latin word for *praise,* when the final consonant is preserved pure; but such cases must occur under every system of pronunciation.

The existing materials upon Latin pronunciation are sufficiently explicit to teach it better than French can be taught by books alone without the aid of oral instruction; but they have been so effectually perverted and kept out of view by the authors of spurious grammars, that we may meet with respectable teachers of what is by courtesy called Latin, who are not aware of their existence. Those who assert that the pronunciation of this language cannot be ascertained might be deemed honest in their opinions, were the proper length of syllables attended to, this being well ascertained, and the basis of Latin poetry; but spurious rules unknown to the Latin grammarians, have been foisted into poetry as well as prose. (See the second note.)

Some are inclined to reject what is incorrect, but they find bad habits too firmly fixed, although they alter their use of the vernacular, or of a modern language, from day to day when they find themselves in error. If any who are already educated possess a false pronunciation in any language, this should not prevent those still to be educated from acquiring a correct one. In fact, this outline is intended for the learner, for professional students, for such as have occasion to quote sentences or words, and for the use of schools of both sexes where Latin is not taught, but where attention is paid to Etymology, Zoology, Botany, and the sciences generally in which Latin words are freely used.

Although not intended for the proficient, who may be presumed to be acquainted with the subject, some quotations are given in the original, to save the trouble of a further reference.

Illustrations from the Greek have been sparingly introduced, because it is not usual to represent this language in Roman characters, and Greek characters would be of no use to many readers. On this account, when Greek words are quoted, they are generally written with the Roman alphabet, or such characters have been selected from the various forms left to us in Greek inscriptions, as most resemble their Roman analogues. This will account for the preference of the Greek characters, S to Σ, R to P, ε to E, and ọ to Ω.

When illustrations are taken from other languages, they are usually printed orthographically in *italics*, and phonetically in Latin characters, although in some cases the two do not differ. Italic characters are also used where the pronunciation was doubtful, or where it could not be represented by the Latin alphabet, as the Irish word for *silver* (§ 258). For the same reason, illustrative words containing the vowels in *fall*, *not*, and the Oriental cerebrals, &c., had to be avoided. In an elementary work on etymology, which the author is preparing, farther illustrations will be found upon subjects touched upon in this volume.

The Oriental etymologies are not expected to have weight with those who consider them "fanciful," or with those who prefer the superficial Richardson to the philosophic Webster, whose chief defect is his sparing use of "Oriental analogies." An apology ought perhaps to be made for employing etymology at all, since in a recent conversation in a railway car with a student who had just graduated with honor in an American college, he stated that he could perceive no etymological connection between words like the Greek GeRANos and the English CRANe, or between the same GeRanOS and the Latin GRUS.

In the following pages the word *diphthong* is written so as to indicate the pronunciation approved by Mr. Smart; and *k* is used in writing *"celtic,"* because the initial of the word intended to be used is not a sibilant.

COLUMBIA, PA., *Sept.* 1850.

INTRODUCTION.*

§ 1. WHEN a student commences the study of a language with the aid of books, his first inquiry has reference to the power of the characters which represent the words.

2. A character is an arbitrary mark, meaning nothing until it has been assigned to a certain sound made use of in speech. For example,

3. The character H cannot be correctly referred to a sound until we know the alphabet of which it forms a part. In Greek it is a vowel identical with the Roman E; in Russian it represents the N of the Roman alphabet; and in Ethiopic it is equivalent to the French or English syllable za.

4. Before pronouncing a written word, therefore, we must know to what language it belongs, or we may read a Greek trissyllable (APETH) as a dissyllable in Roman characters, which would make apeth out of A-RE-TE; an error which has a strict parallel in the practice of reading Latin as if the letters were those of a transmontane vernacular. Hence a Russian cannot with propriety knowingly confound the H and N, a German the Z and C, or F and V; nor an Englishman the G and J, or C and S of the Latin alphabet.

5. Latin being spoken to a considerable extent among the learned, particularly between the residents of different countries; grammars which profess to teach it, as they must be drawn from the same original source, should correspond in every particular,

---

* The asterisks which precede the numbering of some of the paragraphs, refer to notes in the concluding pages bearing similar numbers.

INTRODUCTION.*

§ 1. WHEN a student commences the study of a language with the aid of books, his first inquiry has reference to the power of the characters which represent the words.

2. A character is an arbitrary mark, meaning nothing until it has been assigned to a certain sound made use of in speech. For example,

. 3. The character H cannot be correctly referred to a sound until we know the alphabet of which it forms a part. In Greek it is a vowel identical with the Roman E; in Russian it represents the N of the Roman alphabet; and in Ethiopic it is equivalent to the French or English syllable *za*.

4. Before pronouncing a written word, therefore, we must know to what language it belongs, or we may read a Greek trissyllable (APETH) as a dissyllable in Roman characters, which would make *apeth* out of A-RE-TE; an error which has a strict parallel in the practice of reading Latin as if the letters were those of a transmontane vernacular. Hence a Russian cannot with propriety knowingly confound the H and N, a German the Z and C, or F and V; nor an Englishman the G and J, or C and S of the Latin alphabet.

5. Latin being spoken to a considerable extent among the learned, particularly between the residents of different countries; grammars which profess to teach it, as they must be drawn from the same original source, should correspond in every particular,

* The asterisks which precede the numbering of some of the paragraphs, refer to notes in the concluding pages bearing similar numbers.

recommending a uniform mode of pronunciation, whether printed at Санкмпемербурb, المدينة or 廣東.

6. Latin is called a dead language, and on this account(!) some pretend that they are at liberty to give it the sounds which happen to be represented by similar characters in their own vernacular; a practice which would result in as many jargons as there are perversions of the Roman alphabet.

7. By mispronunciation, much of the value of Latin is lost to etymology and general philology, both of which depend, to a great extent, upon the accuracy with which words can be recalled by the aid of appropriate characters.

8. The use of Latin for philological and conventional purposes renders a uniform conventional pronunciation necessary when it is brought to life in oral discourse.

9. This would prevent ambiguity between certain words; as SŪRCŬLŬS a *twig*, CĪRCŬLŬS a *circle;* SEDO to *calm,* CEDO to *yield;* SCANDO to *climb,* ASCENDO to *mount;* SCĔLESTĪ *wicked,* CŌELESTĪ *heavenly;* SĬLĬCEM a *flint,* CĬLĪCEM of *Cilicia;* CAELŪM a *chisel,* COELŪM *heaven;* INGĔSSĪ I have *carried into,* INJĒCĪ I have *thrown;* and many others.

10. Many languages, as the Russian, Armenian, Georgian, Arabic, Greek, &c., are not written in the Roman character, a fact overlooked by such grammarians as confine their superficial directions to those whose vernacular is supposed to be represented by the Latin alphabet; without giving a Greek or Arab any idea of the subject.

11. Having a rule before him which requires the imposition of vernacular barbarisms, and even forbids a uniform mode of pronunciation, the Russian cannot do otherwise than turn his Latin B into *v* or *f,* and Latin H into *n,* as if there were neither *b* nor *h* in the language; whilst

12. The Greek is forbidden to pronounce XERXES as he usually does, namely CSERCSES, although he is told that the Roman X is CS. Nor must he make Ch identical with his own *Chi,* although he knows this combination was made expressly for it.

13. Philological relations were not taken into consideration by those who, instead of endeavoring to ascertain the true power of

the alphabetic characters, fancied that they must be identical with such as resemble them in their own alphabet; confounding the Russian C and Armenian U (Roman S), or Coptic T (pa), or English J, or French J, or Cherokee J (ɢᴜ, § 240), with the Roman characters of the same form.

14. Whilst some of the Latin characters have been corrupted, they are preserved pure as Greek letters, the initial of the logograph of cȳᴅōɴ being pronounced correctly when it is considered Greek, but confounded with that of sīᴅōɴ when spoken of in a Latin connection.

15. Probably no one acquainted with the subject pronounces the character C differently in the Ànglosaxon (a dead language) from the power it still bears in Gaelic and Welsh, or the word *kirk* would cease to resemble its original cŷʀc. So the Welsh and Scotch word *cist*, the Irish *cisde*, the German and Danish *kiste*, Swedish *kista* and Arabic *kis*, correspond with the Greek κιϛτη and the Latin cīsᴛx. In English, these have been developed into *tshist*, and its literary corruption *tshest*.

16. The English word *poop* (of a ship) is the first syllable of the Latin word pūppĭs; the Swedish, English and Dutch word *kink* is the first syllable of the Latin word cīɴcᴛūᴍ; the English word *croak* is the root precisely of the Latin word cʀōcɪo; and the German term for *emperor* [ᴋᴀɪsᴇʀ] differs little from its original cᴀᴇsxʀ, which the Romans also wrote [cᴀɪsᴀʀ]. See note to § 165.

*17. It is an important law in the interchange of consonants of different contacts, that a guttural, as *k*, readily changes to a palatal, as *s*, but not the reverse. Hence

*18. We falsify a fundamental law of philology, if we assert that a word which contains a guttural, has been derived from one whose corresponding letter was a palatal, as *kist* from *sista, canker* from *canser*, the Greek form ᴋɪᴋϝʀоɴ from the English name *Cicero*, or the English words *keep, kin, kitchen*, from the Anglosaxon *cepan, cyn, cycene*, if these contain a palatal. No one pretends that *cover* (from *couvert*) in its local form (§ 77) *civer*, has an initial *s*; that the biblical logographs [Kedron, Eliakim] are

not identical with [Cedron, Eliacim], or that the anatomical term *sacciform* is pronounced *saxiform*.

19. The reading of Latin should be the successive enunciation of the power of each letter, which would make it strictly phonetic, as it was among the Romans.

20. When in certain words the dipthong AU (in *brown*, German *braun*) was replaced by the vowel O, *the orthography was changed*, as in O-LLX, which had been previously AULX, and in SŪFFŎCO *to suffocate*, from FAUX the *throat*. So when DE NŎUŎ or DE NOVO became contracted, it was written DENUO.

*21. That this was a point of pronunciation is proved by Festus; who also states that the rustics pronounced ORUM for AŪRŪM. In some cases the pronunciation was not uniform, as in LAUTUM and LOTUM, CAUDEX and CODEX, CLAUDO and CLUDO.

22. Thus we find at the beginning of the 5th century a tendency towards a change which has been consummated in French; but the French still write *au* instead of the proper character *o*, contrary to the correct usage of the Latin alphabet.

23. That the vowel O replaced the dipthong AU in a dialect of Italy, is no excuse for the French perversion of the latter, because the Romans did not usually follow the practice of the Greeks in writing their dialects. Cicero, however, wrote as he spoke, when his pronunciation differed from the general standard. §§ 89, 96. Some English authors, as if to justify their Latin cacophony, imagine the English consonant combination *dzh* might have been known in Italy (§ 230); but whether or not, the fact should have no influence in reading Latin, for the reason just given.

24. Were such perversions proper, we might with the Sabines replace H with F in HĪRCŬS, HŌRDĔŬM, or read an initial H in ADRĪANŬS when it is omitted in the writing.

25. The following rules for reading Spanish (from Cubí's Grammar) are well adapted to Latin reading: "To sound every vowel fully and distinctly, leaving, as it were, the consonants to take care of themselves. Never to pass over the small words, but to pronounce them clearly and distinctly. Never to give a very strong emphasis to any particular word in the sentence; for, as every word is fully pronounced, there is not much room for particularizing any one with uncommon vehemence."

ELEMENTS

OF

LATIN PRONUNCIATION.

---

1. OF THE ALPHABET.

*26. An alphabet is a collection of the characters representing the vocal elements in a language. The term alphabet is also used as a name for the aggregate of the vocal elements, which are termed *letters* by Priscian, who, about the year A. D. 525, wrote a voluminous Latin grammar extending to 900 pages. He says that a letter is a sound—the smallest portion of the voice; and the written characters he considers representations of the letters. Other ancient authors use the word letter as synonymous with character.

27. The Latin alphabet has varied in extent at different times. Some modifications were introduced to assist in representing words taken from the Greek, and it is to be presumed that those who introduced them gave them the proper pronunciation; because in most cases, when the words had become naturalized, the foreign characters gave way to the Roman ones.

*28. The division of characters into capital and small letters is scarcely admissible in Latin typography, and Priscian makes no mention of them in writing. The small letter alphabet being used for its convenience in transcribing, lost its peculiar value when printed.

2

29. In the more ancient manuscripts, there was not so much dissimilarity as at present between the two kinds of characters, as in the case of the small B, F, G, L, N, R, T, I (without a dot); whilst the small d, h, m, q, u, y, did not differ materially from the modern form.

30. According to Priscian there are 23 characters in the Latin alphabet. These are A B C D E F G H I K L M N O P Q R S T V X Y Z. To these the moderns have added J and U.

31. Strictly speaking, C, K, Q, are not distinct Latin letters. Some of the old grammarians do not consider X a letter; some improperly reject H as an *aspirate,* and others S as a *hiss.* They might as well have rejected Thi as a *lisp,* and F as a *puff.*

*32. The names of the characters are given by the ancient Latin grammarians, except those of Greek origin, and N when it represents its power in the English word *anger.*

33. The character K (and also Q) is a duplicate of C; X of CS and GS; Z of SD; and ꝏ of PS. Some of the characters, as Ʊ, K, ꓲ, Ⅎ, ꓛ, were rarely used; whilst Ch, Rh, Ph, Th, Y, Z, are of Greek origin.

34. In the following version of the alphabet the duplicate characters are introduced, as well as the representatives of such Greek sounds as are represented in it, although foreign to the Latin language. The alphabetic order of the Greek equivalents is indicated by the numbers.

Characters.	Name in *Latin* and *English.*		Greek equivalents.
[1] A	A	Ah .	[1] A, α
[2] Ʊ	. .	. . .	
[3] B	Bᴇ	bay	[2] B, ϐ, β
[4] C	Cᴇ	cay	[13] K, ϰ
([25] .... Ch	Cʜɪ	. . .	[27] X, χ
[5] D	Dᴇ	day	[4] Δ, δ
[6] E	E	a	[8] H, η *long.*
[7] F	ᴇF	ayf]	[5] E, ε as in *end.*
[8] G	Gᴇ	gay	[3] Γ, γ, ʃ
[9] H	Hᴀ	hah	[10] ʿ
[10] I	I	e	[12] I, ι
[11] J	Jᴏᴛᴀ	yota	I, ι
[12] Ⱶ	. . . .	. . .]	[9] ει
[4'] .... K	Cᴀ	kah	[13] K
[13] L	ᴇL	ail	[14] Λ, λ
[14] M	ᴇM	aim	[15] M, μ
[15] N	ᴇN	ain	[16] N, ν
[16] Nɢ	. . .	ayng	ʃ, γ
[17] O	O	o [ŏ	[18] O, o
[18] P	Pᴇ	pay	[19] Π, π, ϖ
([26] .... Ph	Pʜɪ	. . .	[26] Φ, φ
[4''] .... Q	Cᴜ	coo	[21] ϙ
[19] R	ᴇR	air	[22] P, ϛ, ρ
([27] .... Rh	Rho	. . .	ῥ
[20] S	ᴇS	ace	[23] Σ, ς, σ
[21] T	Tᴇ	tay	[24] T, τ
([28] .... Th	Tʜᴇᴛᴀ	thayta	[11] Θ, ϑ, θ
[22] U	U	oo	ΟΥ, ȣ
[23] V	Vᴇ	way	ȣ
[24] Ⅎ	Dɪɢᴀᴍᴍᴀ	βαυ	[6] Ϝ, β
.... X	ɪCS	eecs	[17] Ξ, ξ
([29] .... Y	Y	. . .	[25] Υ, υ
([30] .... Z	SDᴇᴛᴀ	sdayta	[7] Z, ζ, ʒ
.... Ɔc	ᴀɴᴛɪsɪɢᴍᴀ	. . .	[28] Ψ, ψ
	Yᴀᴅᴇ,	ϛαυ	[20] ꟁ
		ō	[29] Ω, Ꞷ, ω

35. Scheme of affinities between the vocal elements in Latin.

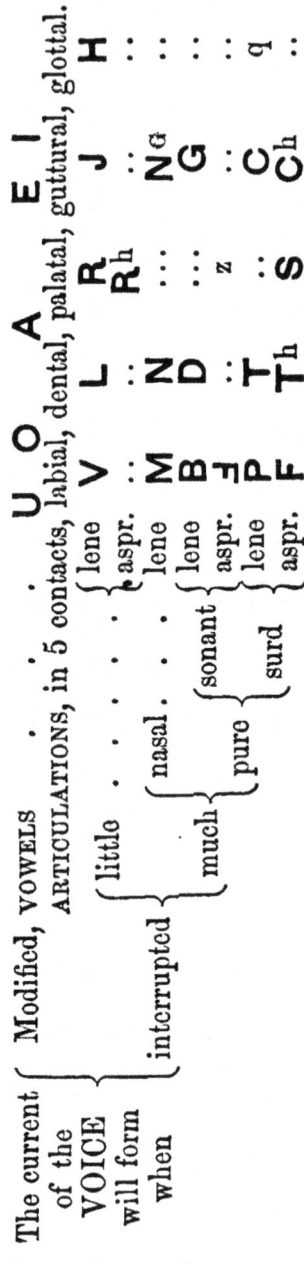

*36. In the foregoing scheme the consonants of the respective contacts are represented in vertical columns, whilst those having certain qualities in common, are indicated in the transverse lines. It will be found of service in studying inflections and euphonic changes, not only of the Latin, but of other languages when the letters belonging to them are properly distributed in it.

37. Elements or sounds of the same contact interchange most readily; and after them, those of adjoining ones. For example, R being the liquid of the palatal contact, is readily interchangeable with s, as in the double forms ARBŎR ARBOS; HŎNŎR HONOS. So ŌS becomes ŌRĬS; AES AERĬS; HAERĔO HAESĪ; but AESTAS makes AESTATĬS; ŪRO ŪSSĪ become ŪSTŪM, taking the next contact, T and S being made nearly at the same point. A similar law appears in the connection between TŪBĔR a *knob*, &c., and TŬMŎR a *swelling*; M being a nasal B, as N is a nasal D. The dropping of M in RŪMPO to form RŪPĪ, is paralleled in SCĪNDO, SCĬDĪ.

---

2. OF THE VOWELS.

38. The Latin vowels are either long (marked ¯) or short (marked ˘), the former being double the length of the latter, according to the ancient grammarians.

.*39. The power of the Latin vowel characters is heard in pronouncing the following English logographs, or written words, in which they appear.

> A is *long* in Ārm, *short* in Ărt.
> E   "   thEy   "   Eight.
> I   "   marIne "   deceIt.
> O   "   Own   "   Obey.
> U   "   fOOl   "   fUll.

40. "The sound of the long vowels was that of the short vowels doubled."—*G. Walker,* in Scheller's Latin Grammar. "The sound of the long and short vowels, though *elementarily the sàme,* were always distinguished in length."—*Scheller.*

41. In Latin it is rather the syllable than the vowel which is long or short, or the subject of quantity.

42. Two consonant characters (excepting H) following a vowel character, usually make a syllable long "by position." Words like CŌNSŪMO to *waste*, and CŌNSŪMMO to *accomplish*; VĪTA *life*,

and vītta a *band,* are distinguished by doubling the consonant where its character is doubled.

43. Dipthongs are long. A vowel preceding another is usually short (even when separated by h), as in cháŏs *chaos,* còpĭa *plenty,* mĭhĭ *to me.* The quantity of vowels, which is long or short at the pleasure of the poets, is called *common.*

44. In old Latin, instead of the mark of length, the vowel character was doubled, as in paacem for pācem. Afterwards the succeeding consonant character seems to have been sometimes doubled for the same purpose.

*45. A doubled character indicated a long syllable, because every addition increases the time, as in the double forms tantŭlŭs, tantĭllŭs; pālātīnŭs, pāllātīnŭs; although there was possibly but little if any difference in the pronunciation of certain words written with a single or double consonant character, as in the forms lītĕrā and littera; āpūlĭā and appūlĭā; bālīstā and ballīstā; causā and caussa; nūmŭs and nummus; bāccā and baca; bellŭā and belua. § 19.

46. In the Teutonic languages a doubled consonant character marks a *short* vowel, so that there is a tendency to pronounce the first syllable of words like pennā, &c., as if it were the English syllable *pen.* This fault should be carefully guarded against. In Latinising Teutonic names, this peculiarity should be rejected.

Accent.

*47. Vowel characters often have the accent indicated by the *grave* (`) and *acute* (´) accentuals in typography; when the former indicates a long and the latter a short syllable, as in màlŭs an *appletree,* and málŭs *bad.* To apply this mode to English, we would write *tárry, stàrry; nàughty, knótty; slàvish, lávish; profàne, profánity.* The acute accentual only is preserved in inscriptions.

*48. In dissyllables the penult syllable (or second from the end) is accented, as in càssĭs a *helmet;* cánĭs a *dog.*

49. In polysyllables the antepenult (or third from the end) is accented, unless the penult contains a long vowel, when that is accented.

I

50. The most contracted of the primary vowels, that formed with the shortest tube when the vowels are made mechanically, is I. It is heard in the English words marIne, fIeld, and is represented throughout Europe, and in general alphabets, by the Roman character. Its short quantity is heard in the English words *deceit, feet, equal.* "The English *seat* retains the Roman pronunciation of sĭTŭS, that is, *seetus*."—*Webster's Dictionary.*

51. Some give the secondary English and German vowel in *fin, fit, pity,* as the "short" quantity of I, a sound which has a different quality, and is unknown in French. Moreover, "every letter retained an invariable sound."—*G. Walker.*

52. Victorinus describes the vowel I as being made with the mouth nearly closed. It was identical with the Greek I, which "was sounded like the *e* in *mete.* The modern Greeks so pronounce it: and here again the English, in differing from the modern Greeks, differ from all the nations of Europe."—*Pennington on the Pronunciation of Greek*, p. 36.

53. A vowel being a simple sound, the Roman I would not be one if its power were that of English *i* (*ai*, in *aisle*) this being a dipthong or double sound.

E

54. The second Latin vowel is heard when long in ŏBEDĬO, *obey;* VENX, *vein;* VERBENX, *vervain;* and when short, in the English words *freight, hate, eight, weight.* It is long in SECIUS *less,* and short in SĔCIUS *otherwise.*

55. The natural position of E being between I and A, it shows its affinities to each, as in TENĔO, RĔTĬNĔO; LĔGO, DĪLĬGO; BXRBX, ĪMBERBĬS; XPTŭS, ĬNEPTŭS; CXRPO, DĪSC-ERPO; and in the double forms SĪVĔ, SEV̇; XLXMANĪ, ALEMANI; XLEX-ANDRĪX, ALEXANDRĔA; HERCULIUS upon coins, HERCŭLĔŭS in stone. In English, a similar relation appears in *obEy, obĬdient.*

56. Varro considers E the vowel in the cry of the sheep (BEE), so that it cannot be the English *e.* The character E is recognized with the Latin power in Europe, and when it is dropped for I,

the character changes with the sound. Thus the Latin SĔCŪRŬS has become SICURO in Italian, as CREATŪRA and ALLĔVO have become CRIATURA and ALLIVIAR in Spanish.

57. As the short and long sound of E differ only in length, they readily flow into each other, as in PRĔHENDO, VĔHĔMENS, which, by dropping H, take the form PRENDO, VEMENS.

*58. The power of I and A being determined, there is no character left for the vowel in *vein* except E.

59. The natural order of the primary vowels, as determined mechanically, is I E A O U or U O A E I, as heard in the English words *field, vein, far, owe, ooze.* This order should be so well impressed upon the memory that the vowels may be repeated fluently in either direction, as it will be found useful in studying the inflections of words; and on this account the elements are here treated according to their affinities.

60. The *fundamental* vowels are the guttural I (in *field*), the palatal A (in *far*), and the labial U (in *ooze*). The closeness of aperture in I and U approximates them to the nearest consonants, into which they are apt to fall, the first into the liquid or semivowel of the guttural, and the last to that of the labial contact. E and O exhibit in a less degree the tendency to become consonants; whilst A, from its openness, and its want of relation to the extreme vowels, is farthest removed from the consonants, and is consequently the type and most noble of the vowels.

A

61. As with all the vowels, the power of A is its name.

62. The almost universal power of the first character of the Roman alphabet is heard when long in FAR *a kind of wheat;* FAS *right,* and in the Latin and Italian word AMO. It is short in ΧΡΑΡ the river *Saone,* in the final of ARMX, ΑΡΞ, and in the English word *ărt.*

63. The French â (as in âme) approaches A, but is not so *open,* that is, the mouth is less open in its formation. Standing in the middle of the vowel series, A is the most open of the whole, and its use gives great power to Italian vocal music. It is equivalent to the Greek A, which Dionysius of Halicarnassus properly

calls the most agreeable of the long vowels, and which is made, as he informs us, with " the mouth as much opened as possible."
—*Pennington*, p. 28. "It seems clear from the description of Dionysius, that this letter was pronounced as we sound the A in *father*. The modern Greeks so sound it, as do most, if not all, the other nations of Europe. Our English mode of pronouncing the Greek A is peculiarly unfortunate, excluding the very sound which Dionysius thought the most agreeable."—*Pennington*, p. 34.

64. The descriptions of the Latin authors agree with the above, as in the expression RICTU PATULO of Victorianus Afer and Terantianus Maurus; and in the HIATU ORIS of Marcianus Capella.

65. There is no evidence to show that in becoming short, the quality of any vowel varied, as in that case it would be a different vowel. §§ 40, 51. The author of "Living Latin" (London, 1847) says, p. 11—"That the Latin vowels have only one sound each, long or short, is clear from Priscian, who, when he would enumerate the varieties of sound which they admit, mentions only those of accent and aspiration, which are merely varieties of its accidents, not of the sound itself." Yet this author, instead of perceiving that the *a* in the English words *ărt, Căiro, kite (kăit)* is short when compared with that in *āye, āh, cār*, gives a vowel scarcely known except in English; namely, that in *fat*, which, so far from having a quantitative relation to the vowel in *arm*, has both a long and short quantity of its own, as in Welsh, where *bāch* (*ch* as in German) means *little*, and *băch* a *hook*.

O

66. The Latin O is heard when long in the English words *owe*, *moan, lo;* and when short, in *obey, ocean, note, invoke* (vŏco). It is found in the Latin words ō!, ōmĕn, sōl (the *sun*, preserved in Swedish and pronounced like the English *soul* or *sole*) ōcĕanŭs, ŏccŭbō, ōcto, ōtĭōsŭs, ōro, ōrno, ōs, ōbnōxĭŭs, quōmŏdo, hŏdĭe, jŏvĭs, jŏcŏr, ŏlŏr, ŏdŏr, ŏbŏrĭŏr, ŏb, ŏdĭum, rŏtx, dĕmŏphŏōn son of THESEUS. It is long in MŌRARI *to be foolish*, and short in MŎRARI *to delay;* long in CYCLŌPS and short in CECRŎPS. It is found in the Spanish words señor, Colorado, and in the German *pol, lob, los.*

67. The round form of the character (O) was intend to picture the lips in forming the sound; a form which doe not accompany the vowel in *nor, not,* which is less common. Our vowel in *fond* occurs but seldom, if ever, in Arabian, India, or Persian words."—*Jones, Asiatic Researches,* 1, 15.

68. When long, the Latin O agrees with the Greek Ο, in orming which, according to Dionysius of Halicarnassus, "the muth is rounded and the lips disposed in a circle, and the breath sikes upon the extremity of the lips."—*Pennington,* p. 29.

*69. O and U being labial vowels, if the organs commence closing, or assuming their quiescent state before the vodity ceases, a labial dipthong will be formed with each, as gutural ones are formed with I and E under similar circumstances. his has induced the author of "Living Latin" incorrectly to conder the ordinary O a dipthong, and as the Latin requires it to e a vowel, he replaces it with the power in *all, nor.* The expreion of Victorinus answers better to the ordinary O.

70. The interchange of O and U shows a greater affinit;between the two than would be the case with *awe,* which hs a greater affinity with A. Thus NAVĪBŬS, CŌNSŬL, EFFŬGINT, stand in earlier inscriptions NAVEBOS, COSOL, EXFOCIONT. So we have the two forms ŎPĬLIO, ŪPĬLIO; PȲLŎS, PȲLŬS; VOLSELA, VULSELLA, *tweezers.* The Greek proper name HEKABE becme HECOBA in old Latin, and finally HECŬBX, passing through A, ιU, of the natural vowel scale.

71. In some parts of Italy O did not exist, its place bng supplied by U; in other parts U was wanting and replacedby O.—*Priscian.* The O of TOLOSA has become U in its mocrn name *Toulouse;* and MUTINA has become *Modena.*

U

72. The Latin U is long in the English words *pool, cool, roα;* and in the Latin words RŪMŎR, RŪS, CRŪS, LŪNA, LŬX, SŬS, MS, SMPLEX. It is short in the English words *pull, full, root;* ad in the Latin words RŬINA, LŬPŬS, SŬPĔRBŬS, TŬMŬLŬS, RŬBIΘN.

73. The Latin U is recognized with its proper sound ad character throughout Europe; and the position of the organsa

forming it is well described by Capella. It is preserved pure in the llowing geographical names:—

> *Anamour* from ANEMURIUM.
> *Tersoos* ἀ TARSUS.
> *Courtenay* ἀ CURTINIACUM.

7 The character (U) is angular in inscriptions (V): and in old rinting the two forms are used indiscriminately, as in LAITUS, VSUPATUR, VSUM, VT, ACVTVS, DIVISIO, QVINQVE. The more con on, but not universal practice of the present day, is to limit the ounded character to the vowel power.

7. U and O being nearly allied, are interchangeable, as in the old 'orm EPISTULA, ADULESCENS; of EPISTOLA, ADOLESCENS; and n HŬMU, used by Varro for HUMO. The same law appears in ie changes to which the English words *gold, more, Rome, doo floor,* have been subject.

7. U and I (completing the circle of the primary vowels) are interchangeable, as in FAMŬLŬS, FĂMĬLĬA; SĬMŬL, SĬMĬLIS; EX-SŬI EXSĬLĬUM; CŎNSŬLO, CŎNSĬLĬUM; in the old Latin of Scipio's ton, PLOIRUME for PLŪRĬMĬ; in the double forms HIC, HŬC *here;* ILL, ILLŬC *there;* LĬBĔT, LUBET; LĬBĔNTĔR, LŬBĔNTĔR; and in TĔGŬMEN, TEGIMEN, which became TEGMEN.

7. The relation between U and I being organic, their inter-chaĝe is common, as in the English words food feed; brood bre ; blood (formerly) bleed; flew flee; you ye; thou (where it ls not become obsolete) thee; foot feet; rood reed; leward lee.

7. The English corruptions of *you* for U, and *eye* for I, whilst they are disproved by this law, tend greatly to mystify the student who wishes to understand the genius of the Latin language.

7. There was a tendency to elide V, as in the change from AU VISTI, MAVELIM, NEVOLO; to AUDISTI, MALIM, NOLO.

Y

0. Dionysius describes this Greek vowel as pinched or com-pre d, and that it is a labial appears from Capella's description, whh assimilates it to the French *u* or German *ü,* with which the sch ars of these nations consider it identical. Pennington is of

67. The round form of the character (O) was intended to picture the lips in forming the sound; a form which does not accompany the vowel in *nor, not,* which is less common. "Our vowel in *fond* occurs but seldom, if ever, in Arabian, Indian, or Persian words."—*Jones, Asiatic Researches,* 1, 15.

68. When long, the Latin O agrees with the Greek O, in forming which, according to Dionysius of Halicarnassus, "the mouth is rounded and the lips disposed in a circle, and the breath strikes upon the extremity of the lips."—*Pennington,* p. 29.

*69. O and U being labial vowels, if the organs commence closing, or assuming their quiescent state before the vocality ceases, a labial dipthong will be formed with each, as guttural ones are formed with I and E under similar circumstances. This has induced the author of "Living Latin" incorrectly to consider the ordinary O a dipthong, and as the Latin requires it to be a vowel, he replaces it with the power in *all, nor.* The expression of Victorinus answers better to the ordinary O.

70. The interchange of O and U shows a greater affinity between the two than would be the case with *awe,* which has a greater affinity with A. Thus NAVĬBŬS, CŌNSŬL, EFFŬGĬUNT, stand in earlier inscriptions NAVEBOS, COSOL, EXFOCIONT. So we have the two forms ŏpĭlĭo, ūpĭlĭo; pȳlŏs, pȳlŭs; VOLSELLA, VULSELLA, *tweezers.* The Greek proper name HEKABE became HECOBA in old Latin, and finally HECŬBĂ, passing through A, O, U, of the natural vowel scale.

71. In some parts of Italy O did not exist, its place being supplied by U; in other parts U was wanting and replaced by O.—*Priscian.* The O of TOLOSA has become U in its modern name *Toulouse;* and MUTINA has become *Modena.*

U

72. The Latin U is long in the English words *pool, cool, room;* and in the Latin words RŪMŎR, RŪS, CRŪS, LŪNA, LŪX, sŭs, MŪS, sŭpplex. It is short in the English words *pull, full, root;* and in the Latin words RŬĪNA, LŬPŬS, SŬPĒRBŬS, TŬMŬLŬS, RŬBĪCŌN.

*73. The Latin U is recognized with its proper sound and character throughout Europe; and the position of the organs in forming it is well described by Capella. It is preserved pure in the following geographical names:—

> *Anamour* from ANEMURIUM.
> *Tersoos* " TARSUS.
> *Courtenay* " CURTINIACUM.

74. The character (U) is angular in inscriptions (V); and in old printing the two forms are used indiscriminately, as in LAEUUS, VSURPATUR, VSUM, VT, ACVTVS, DIUĪSIO, QVINQVE. The more common, but not universal practice of the present day, is to limit the rounded character to the vowel power.

75. U and O being nearly allied, are interchangeable, as in the old form EPISTULA, ADULESCENS; of ĒPĪSTŎLĂ, ĂDŎLĒSCĒNS; and in HŬMU, used by Varro for HUMO. The same law appears in the changes to which the English words *gold, move, Rome, door, floor,* have been subject.

76. U and I (completing the circle of the primary vowels) are interchangeable, as in FAMŬLŬS, FĂMĬLĬA; SĬMŬL, SĬMĬLĬS; EXSŬLO, EXSĬLĬŬM; CŌNSŬLO, CŌNSĬLĬŬM; in the old Latin of Scipio's tomb, PLOIRUME for PLŪRĬMĬ; in the double forms HĪO, HŪO *here;* ĪLLĪC, ĬLLŪC *there;* LĬBĔT, LUBET; LĬBĒNTĔR, LŬBĒNTĔR; and in TĔGŬMĔN, TEGIMEN, which became TEGMEN.

77. The relation between U and I being organic, their interchange is common, as in the English words food feed; brood breed; blood (formerly) bleed; flew flee; you ye; thou (where it has not become obsolete) thee; foot feet; rood reed; leward lee.

78. The English corruptions of *you* for U, and *eye* for I, whilst they are disproved by this law, tend greatly to mystify the student who wishes to understand the genius of the Latin language.

79. There was a tendency to elide V, as in the change from AUDIVISTI, MAVELIM, NEVOLO; to AUDISTI, MALIM, NOLO.

Y

*80. Dionysius describes this Greek vowel as pinched or compressed, and that it is a labial appears from Capella's description, which assimilates it to the French *u* or German *ü*, with which the scholars of these nations consider it identical. Pennington is of the same opinion, and cites Mr. R. P. Knight as follows: "Perhaps the nearest letter to it in modern alphabets is the French accented U, the sound of which is indeed poor and slender; but such as Dionysius informs us that the Greek Υ was." It is both long and short, as in the name of HȲPSĬPȲLE, a queen of LĒMNŎS.

81. From the form of the character Υ, it appears to have been intended to represent a compressed V (U), and it is correctly preserved for such a sound in Polish, Danish, and Swedish. In modern Greek, as in some dialects of German and French, it has degenerated into I, except in a few words. The sound is unknown to the Italian, Spanish, and Portuguese.

82. To form Y, the organs must take the position for I, the jaw must then be dropped to enlarge the cavity within, and the lips pursed and projected, and made narrower than for U. The resulting sound must resemble U rather more than I. "The unpleasing sound and the ungraceful position of the lips agree with the description of Dionysius."—*Pennington.*

*83. Terentianus Maurus states that the Latin language wants the Greek Υ; and according to Victorinus the Greeks represent U by ȣ. The Y was therefore used by the learned who understood Greek, but was replaced by U and I as the words became naturalized. In old Latin it never appeared, until introduced by pedantry—a cause which has had an improper influence with modern transcribers, so that it is often difficult or impossible to determine the orthography of the ancients.

· 84. Standing between U and I in the natural alphabet, Y readily falls into one or the other (but chiefly into U), as in the forms SYLLA and SŪLLĂ; AMYMŌNE and AMIMONE; ALCYŎNE and ALCIONE; SYMBOLA and SŪMBŎLĂ; CHYTRA and CHŪTRĂ; TȲRO, TURO, and TIRO *a novice;* CȲMA, CUMA, CIMA.

85. The change from Y to U is most frequent, as in TŌRTŬS, TŪNDO, MŪS, SŪS, DŬŎ, CŬPRĒSSŬS, which are from the Greek; and in fact, in the dipthongs, and in the Æolio dialect, (Y) had the power of (U), as in some of the Sclavonic alphabets. On this account, when Y *cannot be pronounced,* it is best replaced with U, and the preceding consonant would be more likely to be preserved

pure, as in the proper name cȳrŭs, which, as the name of an Asiatic river, has become cūr or *Koor*.

86. In fewer cases the Greek ϒ has become I, as in stĭpĕs, sxtĭrx, stĭlŭs. Sometimes Y has been improperly placed in regular Latin words, as in sīlvx, pēnsīlvxnĭx, hĭems, tīrō, clĭpĕŭs, lacrĭmx (§ 283), pxpīrĭus, pĭrūm.

87. Instead of perceiving that the interchange of allied vowels is organic, Scheller propounds the erroneous opinion that U was pronounced like O (§§ 71, 75) and the Greek ϒ, citing sulla from syllas as an example of the latter.—*Lat. Gram.*, 1, 16. Now it is evident, that being unable to pronounce the Greek sound, it was naturalized by the use of U, as in the case of duo, &c.

88. Scheller, on the strength of the two forms vertex and vōrtex, states that E was pronounced as O; a view which a foreigner might take of the allied English words *vertex* and *vortex*. Cellarius (*Orthogr. Latina*) considers the word hĭems *winter* as not of Greek origin; whilst Scheller not only asserts it, but insists that it should be spelt [hyems], as if Y could not have changed in so common a word (§ 86). In ancient inscriptions it is spelt with I.

Ⱶ

89. This character, according to Priscian, Donatus, and Velins Longus, was proposed by the Emperor Claudius for a vowel represented by the characters U and I, but in which they had not their true power. Among the words cited by the ancients as containing it, are maxumus (preferred by Cicero) or maxĭmŭs; proxumus or prōxĭmŭs (and doubtless all superlatives), pōssŭmŭs, vōlŭmus, nōlŭmus; artĭbus; mxnĭbūs; aurufex or aurĭfex; mxnŭbĭae or manibiae, vĭr, xucŭpĭum or aucipium.

90. The vowel Ⱶ was probably that in the English words *it*, *fit*, *in*, *pin;* a distinct vowel which is long in Sclavonic and Turkish, and whilst it is allied to I, approaches U by being formed with a more open aperture.

91. Priscian states that short I followed by d, t, r, m, x, seems to have the power of Greek ϒ, as in vĭdĕo, vĭtĭŭm, vīm, vīrtūs, vīx; but we do not know the power of ϒ in his day, its

3

true power being expressly stated not to have occurred in Latin; and it was already provided with a character.

92. Victorin, whilst he mentions those who consider this vowel "thicker" than I and "thinner" than U, recommends the examples in which it occurs to be written and pronounced I, a mode which has prevailed. It is probable that many pronounced these words with pure U or pure I (§§ 76, 77), as Velius Longus states that AVRĬFEX sounds better with I and AVCŬPARE with U.

Ʊ

93. This character occurs in an ancient inscription, replacing final A in the word DICATA. Its power may have been that of the vowel in *further,* or the final one in *comma, altar.* In the volume on Philology of the U. S. Exploring Expedition, Mr. Hale uses this character for this sound.

[Ɛ]

94. It is not likely that the Greek *epsilon* occurred in Latin, where it was always replaced by E, as well as the *eta* (§ 135). This vowel is heard in the English words *fen met,* and is long and a little more open in the French word *même.*

95. The final vowel in HĔRĔ or HĔRĪ *yesterday,* according to Quinctilian, was neither pure E nor I. It was probably the dipthongal sound EJ (§§ 133–4), condemned by Velius Longus as a mispronunciation in TĪBI (TIBEJ); a sound which arose in the Gothic forms AKEJT, AVRKEJS; borrowed from the Latin words ăCĒTŬM *vinegar,* and ŪRCĔŬs a *pitcher.*

*96. This form is not rare in inscriptions, as in the words SĪ, ŬBI, ĬBI, SĬNĔ; which stand SEI, UBEI, IBEI, SINEI; and the termination IS occurs as EIS. Cicero is said to have written CĪVEIS for CĪVĬS, OMNEIS for ŌMNĬS, &c., this being probably a dialectic variation.

[O]

97. There is no evidence that the vowel in the English words *on, not,* and French *mol, noce,* was found in Latin, and no author asserts that (O) had a second power, even in the dipthong ŌI (§ 67).

3. OF THE NASAL VOWELS.

98. An examination of the Indo-European languages from a period long anterior to the Greek might induce us to suspect the occurrence of nasal vowels in Latin. Thus we find the Sanscrit originals of the Latin words DŌNŬM, Sanscrit DĀNA (in Roman characters), ĀNTRŬM (ANTRA) to have a final nasal vowel.

99. The ancient Latin grammarians are sufficiently explicit on the subject of nasal vowels, which they associated with *m,* as in the Portuguese of the present day, where (*bom*) is equivalent to the French (*bon*). In English, nasal sounds are often associated with *ng,* as in (*bong*) for the French (*bon*). In Polish, a mark somewhat like a comma forms an appendage beneath the character.

100. A nasal vowel, like a nasal consonant, is made by pronouncing the letter with the nasal passage open.

*101. Prise-ian makes a distinction between *m* final, initial, and medial. In the first it is *obscure* (that is, *nasal*), in the second with its ordinary power; and when medial, as in ŪMBRX, it probably had its ordinary power, in addition to nasalizing the preceding vowel.

102. Verrius Flaccus indicated the nasality by writing but half the character [M], thus [ʌ], and it retained its place with so little permanency, that VIRO, ANTIOCO,* have been found in inscriptions (the final to be probably understood as nasal) for VĪRUM, ANTIOCUM or ANTIOChUM. So VĒNĔo is from VĒNUᵐ ĔO, and ĀNĬMĀDVĒRTO from XNĬMŪᵐ ĀDVĒRTO. The *m* in CĪRCŪM disappears in CĪRCŬĬTŬS, and QVAMSI (through QVASI) becomes QVXSI.

103. Manutius copies an inscription (p. 143) in which a small curved line (˜) is used (at least by him) to represent M, N and N (*ng*), as in the logographs POENṼ, ĨVICTI, CṼCTARVM, for FOENUM, INVICTI, CUNCTARUM; so that there is antique authority for this mode of graphic representation.

104. In Latin manuscripts and printed books, M (and also N) is frequently indicated by a straight or curved line over the pre-

---

* This final O has become pure in Italian, which is without nasal vowels.

ceding vowel character;* but this is inconvenient, as such a mark interferes with the placing of the accentuals and marks of quantity. On this account, when nasal vowels are to be illustrated, I adopt as near a modification of the Polish mode of indicating them as ordinary typography affords, a mode which is no novelty in Latin typography.†

105. The Latin nasal vowels are I E A O U, as in ĔNĪ͟ᵐ, DĔCĒ͟ᵐ, TĂ͟ᵐ, FLŎVĬO͟ᵐ (§§ 71, 75), TŪ͟ᵐ.

106. The nasality may have been also associated with (N), as in QVŎTĬĒS from QVOTIENS, and the inscriptive forms COSUL or COS. for CŌNSŬL, and COJUX for CŌNJŪX. The letter in question is omitted in the first syllable of the Greek form of CŌNSTĂNTĪNŬS and in HŌRTĒNSĬUS. The Latin word CŌNSPĪRĀRE appears in Italian under the two forms *conspirare* and *cospirare*.

------

4. DIPTHONGS.

107. As vowels are distinguished from consonants by the amount of *interruption*, it may happen that this may be so small as to leave a doubt as to whether the resulting sound is a vowel or consonant, and this really takes place.

108. The extremes of the vowel scale, ɪ and ᴜ, have a great affinity to the allied consonants or semivowels J, V (English *y* and *w*), and readily interchange with them, and their little difference respectively has deceived good grammarians, as in the case of the English word *well*, which has been asserted to be merely *oo-ell*, as *yard* has been considered as *e-ard*. The syllables *woo* and *ye* disprove such views, as they are not repetitions of a single vowel.

109. But a still closer approximation exists in a pair of *coalescents* intermediate to the semivowels and extreme vowels; and

---

* As in—DĂNORŬ REGŬ HEROŪQUE HISTORIA STILO ELEGĀTI, etc., 1514. (See note 28*d*.)

† This mode, and two forms of the superior circumflex (⌣ and ⌢), are all employed by Casserius, DE VOCIS AVDITVSQVE ORGANIS HIST. ANAT. Ferrara, 1600.

they occur as the final element of dipthongs. Their use in form-ing syllables shows that they are virtually consonants and not vowels, as in the English words *now-we go by-you.*

*110.: According to Priscian, a dipthong is a union of two vowels, *both of which are sounded.*

111. A dipthong is a vowel followed by a coalescent. It is not "a union of *two* vowels in *one* syllable," such a union being impossible. Still less are the English syllables *au (awe)* and *eu (you)* dipthongs, notwithstanding the assertions of thoughtless grammarians to the contrary.

112. Having a consonantal quality and power, the coalescents should be represented by the consonantal form of the characters (I, U) as in CLĀVDĬUS, and PROJN *therefore* (when PRŎĬN is a monosyllable). This would render the rule uniform which re-quires that *a Latin word must have as many syllables as vowels.* Lempriere, in certain cases, very properly indicates the quantity in connection with the *vowel* character, and not with that of the consonant, which plays but a secondary part in quantity.

113. Marks of diaeresis (which separates) and synaeresis (which unites syllables) can be used to advantage, as in PhĀËTŌN when a trissyllable, and PhAËTON when a dissyllable. So DEHJNC would make this word a monosyllable by uniting EJ into a dipthong, the H being disregarded.

114. The Latin dipthongs may be divided into *labial* and *guttural,* from the final element, which may be formed at the *lips* or in the *throat.*

115. The *labial dipthongs* are AV̇, EV̇, OV̇; and perhaps UV̇ and IV̇.

116. AV is heard in the English words *brown, house;* or the German *braun, haus;* and in the AU of most languages using the Roman alphabet.

*117. In Italian there is a tendency to separate the AU as dis-tinct vowels, so that an Italian would pronounce the name of the Persian poet (and correctly, according to Sir William Jones) FIR-DA-U-SI, in four syllables; whilst a German would give three, pronouncing the second like the final of *endow.* In modern Greek the labial coalescent is said to have become the English and French consonant *v* or *f.*

118. The coalescents being represented by the characters (ɪ, ᴜ), it might happen that the aid of their near neighbors (ᴇ, ᴏ) would be sought also, especially if the sounds to be represented *could not be minutely analyzed.*

119. We find this in ᴀᴏʀᴇʟɪᴜs, a false orthography of ᴀᴠʀᴇ-ʟɪᴜs, the reverse being the case in ʟᴀᴠᴅɪᴄᴇᴀ for ʟᴀᴏᴅɪᴄᴇ̄ᴀ. These examples are instructive, as they prove the dipthongal nature of the Latin ᴀᴠ. The Portuguese use both these modes of orthography, as in *pau* or *pao* (*a stick*), which is the first syllable of the English word *power.* The Roman city ᴀᴜɢᴜsᴛᴀ in Portugal is now named *Aosta*, the name of the Spanish city *Sara-gossa* was formerly ᴄᴀᴇSARᴀᴜGUSᴛᴀ, and the river named ᴛɪᴍᴀᴠᴜs is now known as ᴛɪᴍᴀᴏ.*

120. The English syllable *cow* is the first syllable of the Latin, Portuguese, Spanish, and Italian word ᴄᴀᴜsᴀ (but see § 117); and the first syllable of the English colloquial word for a dog's bark, *bowwow*, corresponds with that of the Latin ʙᴀᴜʙᴏʀ.†. This dipthong occurs in the old English word *chowse*, and a person who *chowsed* was named a *Chaucer.*

121. ᴇᴠ̇, the second labial dipthong, is preserved in Portu-guese, where it is written (*eu*) or (*eo*), as in ᴅᴇᴜs, ᴅᴇᴏs (*God*). To pronounce this monosyllable, let the English syllable *day* have the final element of *endow* added, and pure *s* superadded, forming *day-ws*, which scarcely differs from the original Latin dissyllable ᴅᴇ̆ᴜ̆s, and the two would be identical, were the latter rendered monosyllabic by poetic license.

122. In the Welsh form of the same word (Diw) the vowel is that in *fin.* This Welsh dipthong is heard in the Yorkshire and New York dialect of English, as in *endue*, pronounced *endiw*, or *endyiw.*

---

* If the word *echoing* is read as a dissyllable, the vowel *o* is converted into the labial liquid *w*, as in

"And the shrill sounds ran echoing thro' the wood."

† Compare the Greek Ϲαΰζω (Doric Ϲαΰςδω) to *bark, howl.*

123. The allied dipthong with the primary vowel in *field*, is found in Portuguese, as in *rio, riu* (*he laughs*), but this word must not be confounded with the dissyllable *Rio* a *river*.

124. OV̇ forms a dipthong nearly as in the English word *froward* or the old English word *snow*, and when words like PRŎŬT and QUOUSQUE (QUŌ ŪSQUĔ) are compressed to diminish the number of syllables, forming PROV̇T, CVOV̇SCVE, the O retaining its normal power. MOVIMĖNTUᵐ probably passed through MŌV̈MENTUᵐ before it became MŌMĖNTUᵐ. The same change may have happened to PRŌVĪDĒNS in becoming PRŪDĒNS (§ 138), and SŎRŎRĪNUS probably passed through SŎŎRĪNUS, SŎŬRĪNUS, SŌV̇RĪNUS and SŌꟄRĪNUS before it became SŌBRĪNUS.

125. In the Duillian column the word N A V E B OV S occurs for the later NĀVĬBŬS, the OV being combined in a single character by superposition; and in inscriptions we find ABDOVCIT, PLOVS (PLŪS), &c. Schneider considers this OV (as well as EJ) to be a true dipthong.

126. UV̇ probably occurred as a Latin dipthong in the change from JUVENIOR and UVIDUS (JUV̇NIOR, UV̇DUS) to JŪNĬŎR and ŪDŬS.

127. IV̇ seems to be found in the poetical abbreviation of PRĪMĬTĪVUS into PRIMITIV̇S.

128. The *guttural dipthongs* are AJ, EJ, OJ; and perhaps IJ, UJ, YJ, by poetical license. AE and AI, by the concurrent testimony of the ancient grammarians, had the same power, but [AI], the older and more correct orthography was allowed to fall into disuse; so that the words AJMILIUS, QVAJSTOR, AJTERNUS, &c., became AEMĪLĬUS, QVAESTŎR, AETERNŬS, perhaps from a jealousy of the Greeks and their literature. (§ 118.)

129. [AI] is used instead of [AE] when poetry requires two syllables, as in TERRAÏ FRŪGĬFĔRAÏ; affording an argument in favor of the double nature of AE, and proving the inconsistency of the later orthography. [AE] is not employed in GRAIŬS, *Greek*, GRAJŌRỤ̄.

*130. According to Terentianus [AE] had the power of the Greek AI; and according to Varro, in the rural word HEDUS, A was inserted in the towns, making HAEDŬS *a kid*, whence it is evident that AE was a double sound, as in PRAEBĔO, ӼENĔŭs, abbreviations of PRAᴱᴴIBEO, AHENEUS.

131. In Portuguese the Latin orthography is preserved, as in the word *pae* or *pai* (father). This dipthong is represented by [AI] in most of the languages of Europe. In French (as in *faire*), in English (as in *fair*), and in modern Greek the characters [AI] represent a vowel sound. There was a tendency towards this change in the time of Varro, who asserts that whilst some said FAENUS, others said FĒNUS. Dialectically [AI] has its Latin and universal power in French.

132. The few modern authors who consider [Æ] a vowel character, make it the French *ê*, which is the English vowel in *fen* lengthened, without becoming E, as in *fairy*. This word (when properly pronounced) is a lengthened form of *ferry*.

133. EJ differs from the dipthong in *aisle* by having the vowel E as an initial. It may be learned by omitting the final vowel from the English syllables *lay-ye*, which will give the Portuguese monosyllable LEI, *law*. In old Latin the forms NAVEJS, CLASEJS, were used for NĀVĔS, CLĀSSĬS. § 96.

134. EJ is the Latin modification of the classic Greek dipthong εῐ, which finally became the vowel I. It is found in the poetical forms DEJ̇NDĔ, AV̇REJ̇S, PERSEJ̇S, NEREJ̇.

135. Those literary Romans who pronounced the Greek *Chi*, may have used εȷ instead of EJ in words from the Greek; and as the character [ε] is merely a rounded form of [E], and not unknown to Latin typography, there is no objection to it in representing unnaturalized Greek words, by those who believe its power was used by the Romans.

136. OJ has two forms [OE, OI], of which the latter is the more ancient and correct. · Both forms are used in Portuguese, as in [*foe, foi*] *he has been*. OJ was interchangeable with U in old Latin, as in COIRAVIT, COERAVIT, CURAVIT; OJNO (OJNǪ) for UNUM—and with I, as in LIBERUM from LOEBESUM.

137. The vowel in *or* being further removed from U than O is, the change between OJ and U indicates that the O of the dipthong was pure, and the ancient grammarians say nothing to the con-

trary. It is pure and short in the Lɛnàpɛ word (ſ as *sh*) ſáhxmŏjs a *crevish* or *crayfish*.

138. The trissyllable prō-vĭ-dens *provident,* became pro-i-dens, projdens, prodens, prūdēns, *prudent.* proělĭum a *skirmish,* is a contraction of pro ilium; and from the compound word cŏ-ėo *to meet,* we have cōētūs *a crowd.*

139. Having from a false theory (§ 69) given to o the power in *on,* the author of "Living Latin" makes oe rhyme with *boy** instead of *beau-y,* or the first syllable of *co-equal,* if this word is pronounced in two syllables.

140. uj is a dipthong of which the initial is u (*oo*), and the Portuguese are more consistent than the Romans in writing it *ue* and *ui.* The Portuguese monosyllable *fui, I have been,* nearly resembles the Latin dissyllable fŭī. uj is heard in the German word *pfŭi,* with which the English word *buoy* (booy) rhymes.

141. uj occurs in the interjection huj; and in the poetical forms cuj (not cvī, according to the analogy of cuj, cūjŭs) hujc, fujt. Terentianus Maurus and Julius Scaliger regard the final of cuj to be j; and Priscian considers the final of the vocative form caj in the same light.

142. yj may occur in shortening words or inflections like polyidus, imityis, cotyis, capyis, ityi.

143. When yi is followed by a vowel, the coalescent is apt to become a consonant, as in har-py-ia (hᴀr-pȳ-jᴀ), or the French words *essuyer, noyau.*

144. ij may occur like yj, as in livij, used by Ausonius.

145. As the Romans used but a single character for the vowel and consonant power of i and v respectively, errors in pronunciation may occur from inability to determine when the consonantal

---

* "Rightly to find the Latin diphthong œ
 The sound of o and ᴇ you must employ.
 No Roman ever sounded it as we
 Who make the ᴁ and œ like English ᴇ;
 For so our doctors taught us docile boys,
 Not to distinguish between ᴁ's and œ's.
 And thus a hundred errors find their way,
 By this confounding ᴁ and œ with ᴇ."—P. 40.

powers should be employed, as in HŬIC, which might be made
to rhyme with the English word *wick*, destroying the dipthong
by turning U into a consonant. A parallel change would be
made if IU dipthong were changed into the English syllable *you*,
that is, from IV to JU.

146. The union into a single character of [Æ, Œ] is improper,
because it breaks the uniformity of notation, no other vowel characters being so represented. Characters are sometimes united
to economize space upon Roman coins, of which the syllables AV,
ME, NE, ET, VE, TV, VAL, MAR, and others, afford examples. In
forming [VAL], the second line of [A] would be applied to the
top of [V], whilst it would form the stem of [L].

---

5. LABIAL CONSONANTS.

V

147. If the lips be gradually closed upon the vocal current,
the liquid of the labial contact will be formed. Its quality
approaches that of the vowel U so closely, that in Roman inscriptions the two were represented by the single character V, as in
PŪBLĬCV̌S *public*, LĪQVŎR a *liquid*.

*148. The ancient grammarians include B, P, F, M, in the
labials; generally confounding V with U (§ 108); but Cicero
adds V when it has its consonant power. They do not hint that
the consonant is formed differently from the vowel V, so that this
must be the English *we* and not the English *ve*.

149. Those Latin authors who, in treating of the alphabet,
describe F as being formed with the lower lip and upper teeth,
say nothing about V ever being formed in this manner; and the
Greeks, in representing Roman names, make no distinction com-
patible with such a difference, as in VULTURNUS [Οὐουλτοῦϱνος,
ȣλτϱνος (§ 169)], the initial syllable being the English *wool*.

*150. According to Pennington, "The Roman V was more
probably our W," an opinion with which Webster, Donaldson,
Rapp, and the author of "Living Latin" agree.

151. The English syllable *sway* occurs in the second syllable

of MANSVĒTUS *tame*, and in the first syllable of SVĒVUS, but not when it is the trissyllable sŭEVŭs *relating to the Suevi*. TĔNŭĬS *thin*, has three vowels, but when contracted into TENVĬS it has but two. The reverse takes place in SĪLVX, which Horatius uses in three syllables. It is not probable that the *same word* was intended to be as dissimilar as the use of the English letters *u* and *v* would make it.

152. The affinity between U and V is proved by the derivation of NAVTA and CAVTIO from NAVITA and CAVITIO; and by the poetical use of DISSOLUO, EVOLUAM, PERVOLUENT; instead of the trissyllables DISSOLVO, EVOLVAM, PERVOLVENT.

153. Cicero and Plini relate that M. Crassus, hearing a crier of a kind of figs cry CAVNĔAS (usually printed 'cauneas'), took it for a bad omen, understanding the cry to be CXVĔ NE ĕAS, *beware how thou goest*, the first E being probably indistinctly enunciated, and the two others lengthened and confluent (§ 57). The English mode of pronouncing the first syllable of 'cauneas' *caw* and CAVE with English *v*, destroys the analogy between the two forms.

154. In the following examples the Latin *way* has been preserved in English :—

VXLĔO to be *well*.
VXLLŭm a *wall*.
VADO to walk, *wade*.
VXcillo to *wag*, be *fickle*.
VXSTO to *waste*.
VASTXTUS laid *waste*.
VANNO to *winnow*.
VĔRRŭCX a *wart*.
VĬX a *way* or road.
VEHA a *wagon*.
VĔHO to carry, whence *weigh*.
VĬLLŭs *wool*.
VELLŭs a *fleece*.
VĔNTŭs *wind*.

VERMĬS a *worm*.
VĔSPX a *wasp*.
VĬDŭX a *widow*.
VĬGĬLO to *wake*, *watch*.
VINCA a *winkle* (shell).
VŏLO to *will*.
VĬCŭs a village or *wic*.
BERVĪCium *Berwick*.
VĪNŭm *wine*.
VITRŭm *woad*, glass.
VŏLVO to roll or *wallow*.*
VŪLNŭs a *wound*.
VĔGĕo to be strong, to *wax*.
VĪSCŭM glue, whence *wax*.

155. Although the use of the rounded or angular character

---

* *Wheel* is from the same root, namely, the Sanscrit VAJL to *turn*.

[U, V] is almost a matter of indifference in Latin typography, it is better that one form should be invariably used for the vowel and the other for the consonant (§ 112).

156. U, "when followed by another vowel in the same syllable, becomes a consonant and should be written V; as XQVX, SANGVĬS, &c."— *G. Walker.*

157. In a few instances V was dropped after C, as in the word SĔCŪTUS, which had been SEQVUTUS; in the double form SĔQVIUS, and SĔCIUS; and in COLLĬQVĬAE, used by Columella where Plini uses COLLICIAE.

158. If there was no V after Q (as in the French and Spanish *qui*), CUR could not be derived from QVARE, CONCUTIO from QVATIO, CUJUS from QVIS, the Spanish *cuatro*, the Gothic *fidur* and English *four*, &c., from QVATUOR; nor the Spanish *agua* from XQVX. The Greeks represented the Roman name QVINTUS by [KYINTŎS]; and many rejected Q altogether, writing CVIS for QVIS, &c. *See under* Q, §§ 290, 292.

M

159. When the lips are entirely closed and the voice is allowed to pass through the nose, the labial nasal will be the result.

160. M is a nasal B, which accounts for the derivation of GLUMA from GLUBO; and the two forms PRŎBŌSCĬS and PROMUS-CIS. Its relation to V is shown in PRŌMŪLGO to *publish* or *proclaim*, from PRŌVŪLGO, having the same meaning.

B

161. When the lips are closed without opening the nasal passages or stopping the vocality, the sound of B will be given.

162. P had, as far as we know, a uniform power; and as B replaced it, as in the forms REPO, REBO; SCRĪBO, SCRIPO; PȲR-RHŬS, BURRUS; POPLICUS [πѳπλικος in Greek], PŪBLĬCUS; PŌPLĬ-CŎLX; PŪBLĬCŎLX; it is certain that the power of the French and English B existed in Latin.

ꓶ

*163. When the vocal barrier is broken by forcing B through

the lips, a sound will result somewhat resembling the English, French, and Spanish *v*, which latter is a labio-dental, and will be here represented by ᴠ for the sake of illustration.

164. The pure labial consonant ɹ is represented by the German [ᴡ], and by the Spanish [*b*], in certain cases, as in [*Còrdŏbă*], from the Latin cōʀᴅŭʙᴀ. It is probably the Hebrew *bĕith;* and it occurred in Greek, where its character was termed βαυ (properly ɹᴀⱱ̇), or *aeolic digamma*, because its form [ꟻ] resembles a union of two *gamma* characters [ᴦ].

*165. To prevent it from being confounded with their own character for F, the Romans inverted it, as in writing ᴠĭʀ, ᴠīʀᴛŭs, sᴇʀᴠŭs [ɹɪʀ, ɹɪʀᴛᴜs, sᴇʀɹᴜs;] but its use was soon relinquished.

166. The power of ᴠ (English *w*) is usually attributed to ɹ, probably because the German and Spanish sound alluded to (§ 164) is scarcely appreciated as distinct from ᴠi or ʙ.

167. The small Greek letters being more easily written than the capitals, the digamma would be written [ɣɣ], which would pass into [ᴡ], and the origin of the latter character being misunderstood, it was confounded with [ᴜ, ᴠ]. From this it appears that [ᴡ] has its proper value in German. It has no place in the Romish languages, and when it appears in French, in foreign names, its power is that of ᴠ.

168. The Greek and Latin [ʙ], and Hebrew [ב, or כ when aspirate], must have had precisely the unstable power of the Spanish [*b*], sometimes lene or pure, and sometimes aspirate, and when aspirate, forming ɹ and allied to ᴠ. This seems borne out by the Hebrew ᴀʀɴᴀβ*eth*, and Arabic ᴀʀɴεʙ *a hare;* the Greek ᴘʜʀᴀᴛǫʀ, ɢŏᴍᴘʜŏs, and the Macedonian variation ʙʀᴀᴛǫʀ, ɢŏᴍʙŏs; and the old inscriptive forms ʙᴇʀᴜᴍ, ᴘʀᴏʙᴀʙᴇʀɪᴛ; for ᴠᴇʀᴜᴍ, ᴘʀᴏʙᴀᴠᴇʀɪᴛ. § 174.

169. The views taken here elucidate the use of the Greek digraph ου or ȣ (Latin ᴜ) and β, in representing allied or identical Latin words, as in Λαȣϊνιȣ and Λαβινιατων, used by Dionysius in allusion to ʟᴀᴠīɴĭu^m. So we find the name of ᴠᴀʀʀᴏ given as Βαῤῥων and ȣαῤῥων. See note 83.

170. It is a curious fact in connection with these discrepancies,

4

that there are Spaniards who, knowing that their [b] is never v, fancy it is always lene or pure; and I have known it to be insisted upon that the German [w] is identical with the English [w].

171. As ꓩ was used in some words written with [v], this character, as well as [B], probably represented it to some extent; as in the old inscriptive forms DANVVIVS, ACERVVM; for DANUBIUS, ACERBUM.

172. The Greek [B, β] aspirate? became in some cases the Latin v, as in the words vīcĭx, vŏlo, vīvo.

173. The character ꓩ being rejected, its power probably remained associated with [B] as in Spanish; as we find the double forms bĕnĕ, vene; bxsĭs, vasis; lxbŏr, lavor; it being extremely easy for the aspirate ḃ to fall into the allied v, of which an example is furnished by the German words wein, will, when compared with the English words wine, will.

174. The B was probably at first aspirated in words from the Greek having *phi*, as bxlxenă, nĕbŭlă, xlbŭs, ōrbŭs, xmbō.

175. v became B or ḃ, as in bellūm from dv̇ellūm, bis from dvis; and in besica for vēsīcă, larba for lxrvă, berna for verna, &c.

176. B sometimes replaces P, as in absens, xbsŏlūtūm, from the older forms apsens, apsolutum. So we find conlabsum for collapsum.

177. B must have been pure in the numerous cases where it interchanged with P.

P

178. When the vocality of B is stopped, P is the result; it is therefore a surd B, as B is a sonant P. It was not subject to aspiration, which formed a sound foreign to the language.

179. P sometimes replaces B, as in cănōpŭs [Κανωβος]; and in the inscriptive form optinebit for ōbtĭnebĭt, &c. § 162.

180. The character for P arose from the Greek form [Π], the right side of which was frequently made but half the length of the left, forming a character [Γ] to be seen upon old Roman coins.

Ph ꟼꞱ

181. When the breath is forced through the lips (as in blowing a small object), the Greek *phi* [Φ, φ], (a labial *f*) is the result. It is therefore the corresponding surd of the sonant digamma. It is heard in Swedish, and is represented by [*f*] in the German word *kopfweh*. According to Pennington the modern Greeks pronounce [Φ] soft and full, "more like a sigh, though it is not easy to express the difference in writing." P. 71.

182. Phi occurs in certain words of Greek origin, and there is sufficient evidence of its distinctness from F, as in the case of the Greek witness ridiculed by Cicero for pronouncing a proper name PhUNDANIUS instead of FUNDANIUS. If the Greek digraph [αυ] was not AV but AF, as the modern Greeks maintain, Cicero's witness would have had no difficulty with the Roman F.

183. In naturalized words of Greek origin phi became F, as in FĪLĬŬS *a son;* FĀMĂ *fame;* FŬGĂ *flight;* FŪR *a thief;* FĔRO *to bear;* FALLO *to deceive;* FĀGŬS *a beech;* FRĀTĔR *a brother.* In inscriptions we find FÀSĒLŬS *a skiff;* FALĔRAE *trappings;* SIFO *a siphon;* ELEFAS (and ELEPhAS) *an elephant;* DELFINUS *a dolphin,* which the moderns write with [Ph]. The carpensian Virgil and that of the Vatican have SULPUR for SULFUR *sulphur.* The ancient PhAIUM is written [*Faïoum*] or [*Faïoom*] in books.

184. In some cases phi became P, as in PURPUREUS [πορφύρεος], PALANGA or PhĂLANX, PROSERPĬNĂ; in the double form TRUPERA, from TRYPhERA; and in the change from PhOENĬCĬUS *Phenician,* to POĔNĬCŬS, and finally to PŪNĬCŬS *punic.*

*185. Some authors suppose that the Greek PHI (also Rh, Th, and Ch) was P *followed by* an aspirate, as in the English word *ha*Ph*azard,* because the ancient grammarians regard it as P *and* an aspirate, as it is in fact; for if an aspirate is made and the lips be gently closed toward the P position, phi will be formed. Hence this sound is not a post-aspirate, but a co-aspirate P, or this element modified by a synchronous aspiration.

186. Quintilian admired this sound as a pleasant breathing, which shows its nature; whilst Terentian wished it to be pro-

nounced in introduced Greek words, although this could not be
done by the Romans without special instruction.

*187. The power of [F] is known (§ 190), and Priscian de-
scribes it as composed of P *and an aspirate*, so that it is related
to Phi, which is not the fact with P followed by H.   Moreover

188. The Greeks, who could not pronounce F, represented it
by [Φ] phi in Latin names, as in Φαβιος, Φαυςτυλος; for FABĬŬS,
FAV̌STŬLUS.

189. In words borrowed from the Greeks, Phi is sometimes
represented in Roman inscriptions by a character formed of a
union of [P] and the right hand portion of H.   See *Manutius'
Orthogr.*, Venetiis, 1566, pp. 215, 271, in the words NICEPIOR,
PHILEMON.   The former inscription has [TH] united in the word
ΧΜΑΡΑΝΤΗŭs, by adding the horizontal line of [T] to the left
hand line of [H] lengthened upwards.

F

*190. The Roman F is correctly pronounced by the moderns;
as the ancient grammarians describe it as being made with the
aid of the lower lip and upper teeth.   There is no evidence of its
corresponding sonant V existing in Latin; and it is also wanting
in German.

PH, etc.

191. Modern writers on Latin grammar have falsely assumed
that if a Latin word is derived from the Greek it must follow a
certain orthography; and if not derived from this language, it
cannot have PH in it.   It might as well be said that the English
words haPHazard and uPHold are 'incorrectly spelt, because PH
should be placed only in words of Greek origin.

192. The orthography of BOSPHORUS is said to be incorrect,
because the etymology requires it to be BOSPORUS, an assertion
which virtually denies that H can be acquired in words from the
Greek where it is absent, although HIBISCŲ and HELOPS are
examples to the contrary.

193. The word BŌSPHŎRŬS would not be [Βωςφοςος] in Greek

characters, but [Βωςπόϱος], as ISTHUC (IST-HUC) would be [ιςτ'υκ] and not [ιςϑυκ].

194. H followed P, &c., (when written) in TRIUMPHUS, INCHOO, COCHLEA, BACCHUS, and other words.

195. Cicero thought H should be rejected from TRIUMPHUS, PULCHER, CARTHAGO, and CETHEGUS, probably because he did not pronounce it, and his authority is sufficient for its rejection. This fact is sufficient evidence that PH in TRIUMPHUS are not equivalent to F; and the inscriptive forms TRIUMPUS, PULCER, are sufficient authority for its rejection.

196. If this view of the double nature of [H] is correct, there is no means of readily determining when it is to have its independent power. On this account [H] is used when the pure sound is supposed to be represented; and [h], which is an ancient form, when it is merely a diacritical mark of co-aspiration.

---

6. DENTAL CONSONANTS.

L

*197. L is the liquid or half interruption of the dental contact, and the descriptions of Victorinus and M. CAPELLA correspond with the ordinary modern power.

198. L interchanges with the liquid of the next contact R, as in PAVLUS and PARVŭs *little;* PARĪLIA and PALILIA *a kind of coat.* This change is extremely common in the languages of Polynesia, and is observed in the Spanish *esclavo* and the Portuguese *escravo.*

199. L interchanges with D, as in DACRIMA and LACRĬMA a *tear;* ŏDOR an *odour,* OLEO to *scent.*

N

200. N bears the same relation to D that M bears to B.

D

201. D is the sonant, fully interrupted member of the dental

4*

contact. It is interchangeable with T, as in ХРИТ for ĀPŬD, SET for SĔD. This change corresponds with that of P to B. § 179.

T

202. T is a surd D, or D deprived of its vocality.

Th

*203. Th is an aspirate, usually, but not necessarily formed a little in advance of the ordinary position of the dental contact, like the Irish *d* in certain cases. It is the equivalent of the Greek theta, which the modern Greeks pronounce as in the English word *thin*.

204. When Th replaces S it forms a *lisp*, and this interchange indicates the co-aspirate nature of theta [Θ, Ϩ] as in Thɛŏs *god*, in the Doric dialect Sɛŏs, and in the Laconian SIŎR. § 220.

205. The Germans, French, and Italians are not familiar with the sound of Th, and they accordingly replace it with T, which the author of "Living Latin" justifies.

206. The English sound of [Th] is common in the Oriental languages, and so is H following T, as in *foo*THo*ld*.

207. The Sanscrit T remains T in Greek and Latin, and D and T followed by H become Th, and also T in Greek; which is in favor of the post-aspirate theory that theta represented the T and H in *po*THo*ok*. But

208. The Sanscrit D followed by H becomes the Greek delta [Δ, δ] to which the modern Greeks give the power of Dh in *this*. Moreover, the Sanscrit pure T also becomes the Greek theta, which is against the post-aspirate theory.

209. The post-aspirate theory would remove an anomaly from the Latin alphabet, namely, the representation of a single sound by two characters, but language must not be sacrificed to writing.

210. By taking [Th] as the representative of two sounds, as in *penthouse, Beethoven;* or of T alone, as in *isthmus, Thomas, Anthony, Luther, Rothschild, Othello,* we establish a rule which must be followed with [Ph] and [Ch].

*211. H occurs after T in ISTHUC, ISTHIC, ANTHAC (when ANTĒHAC is condensed), PŌSTHAC, POSTHŬMUS *posthumous*, and probably in, PENTHEMĪMĒRIS (from the Greek PΕNTΕ HEMI MΕRIS).

(𝑤)

212. The modern corruption of reading the English *sh* instead of T in words like LĒCTĬO a *reading*, RXTĬO *reason* [and of Cay in ōCĒXNŭS *ocean*) is improper; and a rejection of *sh* implies that of the Italian corruption *tsh*.

*213. Saint Hjerom (who died A. D. 420), after stating that the Hebrew Samech is S, finds himself unable to give his Latin readers an idea of the Hebrew 𝑤 (or 𝑤) *shin* (or SIN as he was compelled to write it), because the sound does not occur in Latin.

214. According to the same authority the Hebrew ʏadde (usually but improperly read as *ts*) is disagreeable to Roman ears. It is a peculiar aspirate consonant of a quality between English *sh* and ch (χ), and equivalent to the Arabic *sad*, and Greek ςαμπὶ or ÇAN, whose place in the Greek alphabet is next after π.

---

7. PALATAL CONSONANTS.

R

215. R, the liquid of the palatal contact, must be trilled or vibrated to make it agree with the descriptions of the ancients. It cannot therefore be replaced with the English smooth *r*. It sometimes interchanged with L, as in PXTĔRX and PXTĒLLX.

Rh

216. Rh, the aspirate of R, is surd or whispered. It is used almost exclusively in words taken from the Greek, which gets the sound from the Oriental languages. In the Romic languages it is preserved in the French terminations *pre tre cre.*

217. The Greek aspirate R (ς‘) was not always preserved in Latin derivatives, as in RŎSX *a rose*, RESĪNX *resin;* being, like other foreign sounds, rejected from properly naturalized words. The old Latin word BURRUS, which was legitimately developed

from the Greek, was afterwards considered a Greek name and replaced with PYRRHUS.

S

218. s, in French and English, when it occurs between two vowels, is apt to be affected by their vocality, and to become sonant, as in *miserable;* and we might hence incorrectly conclude that the rule is universal.

219. In Spanish, s preserves its pure hissing power, and as the ancient grammarians do not mention a sonant power, the same sound must be preserved, as in the English syllables *say* (SE *himself*) *ace* (ĔS *thou art*). The Latin word TRES *three*, is preserved in Spanish, and pronounced like the English word *trace*, which is a little shorter than the Latin word.

220. s was interchangeable with its liquid, as in the old forms PLISIMA for PLURIMA; QVAESUMUS for QVAERIMUS, § 76; PAPISIUS for PAPIRIUS; LASES for LARES; ASAS for ARAS; MELIOS for MELIOR; FUSIUS for FURIUS; and FASENA by the Sabines, for ARENA.

Z

221. z, which (like Y) was not used in old Latin, is a double letter according to the ancient grammarians, and it accordingly lengthens a syllable by "position."

222. z is composed of s and D, but we are not informed whether the hissing (surd) or buzzing (sonant) sound was used. In the vocal scheme (§ 35) the latter is assumed.

*223. According to Dionysius, z is composed of s followed by D, "and that this is done advisedly appears from a passage in Herodian." (See the note.)—*Pennington*, p. 70. According to Maximus Victorinus z is SD, the proper name MEZENTĬŬS being MESDENTIUS; and in consonance with this view, the proper name EZRA or EZRAS is given as εσδρας (ESDRAS) by Origen. The ancients named D a *mute* and s a *semi-vowel*, and Verius Flaccus (if the text is pure) says that without doubt z ends with a mute. The Dorians wrote [SD] at length, instead of [Z], as in [MεLISDŎ] for [MεLIZǪ], so that SD is correct, at least as far as the Doric dialect is concerned.

*224. Surd consonants being less difficult to form than sonant ones, they may be expected where the latter occur. The Italian *dz* and *ts* are *not Greek combinations,* and were the former included in z, we would still want TS, which should be at least as common as DS. But compound forms like εSDεCHŎMAI show that SD is a Greek combination, although usually represented by [z]; we may therefore *naturally expect its corresponding surd* ST, which we find so common that it has been provided with a character [ς], as in αςϱον (ASTRŎN) a *star;* and words like ςφαιϱιςτηϱιον from ςφαιϱιζω, ςαλπιςτης from ςαλπιζω, κλυςτϱη from κλυζω (κλυςδω), and the double form MASTŌS and MAZŎS (*masdos*) are conclusive. *Characteristics* of a langụage should be faithfully recorded, and none should be relinquished because the development of certain modern languages has taken a different direction.

*225. z, in naturalized Latin words, took one or the other of its constituents, as in MEDENTIUS and MESSENTIUS, instead of MEZĒNTĬŭS; MUSSO, SPISSO; and in old Latin we find the Latinized forms SONA, SEVXIS; of ZŌNX, ZEVXĬS. Replacements like these are also found in Greek, as δδ (lisped?) for z in Doric; and KYPRISMŌS from KYPRIZǪ. Compare φϱαζω, φϱαςω, εφϱαδον.

226. In modern Greek [z] is a vocal s, as in *rose;* and this seems to have been its ancient power (or a dialectic variation) in a few words, as in ZMĪRNX *Smyrna.*—(*Pennington,* p. 69.) This view is confirmed by the variations in inscriptions, as LEZBIA for LĒSBĬX; PHILOGENEZ for PHILOGENES; Φιλοκλῆζ for Φιλοκλῆς.— (*Schneider,* p. 382), although, according to Priscian, no true Greek word ends with z, and Σεὺς for Zεὺς, and BYΣANTION as well as BYZANTION upon ancient coins. So the name of the Spanish town SXGŪNTUS was written with an initial [z] by the Greeks. The English z was probably found in the Eolian ZA for DIA, z and *d* being allied sounds.

227. In Italian, z has become both *dz,* as in LAZARO; and *ts,* as in CALZA; and in this language (and in German) s has crept in between T and IO, as in *nazione,* from NATĬO a *people.*

228. The corrupt mode of reading Latin by inserting s after T

in words like NATĬO and GRATĬX, is supposed to date as far back
as the beginning of the seventh century; as we learn from Saint
Isidor,* of Spain, that JUSTITIA was at that time pronounced
JUSTIZIA, but we are still in doubt whether his z had its ancient
power, its English one, or the Spanish lisp. Lipsius quotes a
passage (p. 74, which Schneider does not consider ancient) in
which TZ is assigned as the power of this T.

229. Latin ceased to be the vernacular language of Italy
towards the end of the sixth century.

(dzh, zh)

*230. A few English authors have endeavored to justify the
English *dzh* in Latin from the word JŪPĬTĔR, which they think
may have had an initial D, being, as they say, derived from DIU
PITER; although others derive it from JOVIPATER, and DIESPITER.
But DIUPITER would merely have produced the first syllable of
the English word *due* (not *jew*), as in ADJUNCTUS, ADJUTO-
RIUM, which have become a*dyu*ntivo, a*dyu*torio, in Spanish. In
a similar manner, the *gay* of the Irish word cuig *seven* (the first
syllable like *coo*, the second as in *i*gnite) changes dialectically to
the Latin DJ, forming CŪ*i*DJ, not *coo-idzh*, which would be an
English development.

231. Moreover, a consonant preceding another was frequently
dropped, as in the proper name BELLIUS from DVELLIUS; in BIS
from DUIS; the English *when* from the Latin QVANDO; the
Dacro-romanic *ava* for AQVA; and the Oscan *pettora* when compared with QVATUOR.

232..As the sonant phase of a consonant is more difficult to
form than its surd equivalent, it cannot be expected that the
Romans, who could not pronounce *shin* (§ 213), would be able
to form its sonant, the French *j* as in *azure*, which is included
in *dzh*.

233. If [T] is another form of [S, *sh*, or TS] in ŌTĬŌSŬS *at
ease;* [D] must be read as English z or *zh*, or be followed by z, in
ŎDĬŌSŬS *hateful.*

---

* Schneider, p. 356. Grotefend, 2, 272.

8. GUTTURAL CONSONANTS.

234. The guttural contact is formed with the base of the tongue and palate.

J

*235. J (yota) is the liquid, or half interruption of this contact. It is heard as the initial of the English words *you*, *yoke*, and in the last syllable of *hallelujah*, which is spelt in English with the proper character, as recognized in Italian, German, Polish, and most of the languages of northern Europe.

236. The natives of JÀFA (written [Yâfa] by a recent English traveler), and "Yebna," the ancient JOPPA, and JAMNIA, preserve the initial of these names pure; and in the Levant the initial of the names *John*, *Jacob*, and *Joseph*, corresponds with the German sound, and no one pretends that the Hebrew originals should be pronounced differently. The river of India named JOMANES by the Romans, is now called JAMUNA (Yamoona) by the natives, and corrupted into *Jumna* by the English.

237. The English pronoun *you* occurs in Swedish, where it is spelt [JU] as *yule* is spelt [JUL], with the proper characters. The English word *young* differs only in the vowel from the German *jung*, which is the Gothic *jungs*, the Latin JUVENIS and the Sanscrit JUVAN, giving the last in Roman characters, the first and third letters being the English [y] and [w]. From the Sanscrit JUGA̱ resulted the Latin JUGU, the Gothic and Dutch JUK, the German JOch, the Spanish *yugo* and the English *yoke*.

238. The consonant J has been retained in many Spanish words of Latin origin, as in *ayunar*, JEJŪNĀRE; *yacer*, JĂCĔRE; *yactura*, JĂCTŪRĂ; *yambigo* (Ital. Jambico) IĂMBĬCUS; *yugular* (Italian Jugulare) JŬGŬLĀRIS; *yuxtaposicion*, JUXTAPŎSĪTIO; *conyugal* (Italian conjugale) CONJŬGIĀLIS.

239. J has to some extent become *dzh* in Italian, as in *giacere* from JACERE; and also G (in the same contact), as in *conghiettura* (Spanish *conyettura*), although *conjettura* is also used. A somewhat similar change has taken place where J has become *ch* in

Spanish, J, G, and ch being members of the same contact, and therefore interchangeable.

240. The Spanish use of the character J to represent ch, is therefore less of an error than to make it the representative of *zh* or *dzh;* just as the character G is less perverted when read J (as in Bohemian and Gothic), than when it is read *zh* as in French, or *dzh* as in English. When [G] represents the Roman [J] it is surmounted by a dot in Irish, as in writing *saigitteoir,* Latin SAGĬTTĀRĬŭs an *archer.*

241. Double forms like ĬŌSEph and JŌSEph; XBĬĒGNŭs and ABJEGNUS *made of fir;* and the use by Plautus in the dative case singular of EJI for EI show the close relation of J and I.

NG

*242. The guttural nasal is heard as a final in the English and German word *sing.* It is represented by [N ADULTERINUM] in Latin, where it occurs before the gutturals C (Q, X) G, and ch, as in ANCŎRX an *anchor,* ANCĪLLA a *maid servant,* ĬNQVĪRO to *inquire,* LŌNGŭs *long,* ANGVĬLLX an *eel,* ANXĭŭs *troubled,* ANChĪSĒS *Anchises,* ANGĔLŭs an *angel,* ĬNGĔNŭŭs *ingenuous,* LONGINUS *Longinus.*

243. The Greeks and Romans neglected to provide this element with a peculiar character. In old Latin it was more correctly represented by [G] in the Greek manner, as in AGGŭLŭs an *angle,* AGGVILLA (AGGULUS, AGGVILLA), the sound having a nearer relation to G than to N, and to represent it by the character of the latter, conveys a false idea of its affinities, as if the character for M were allowed to represent N, this being a parallel case. The change was probably made to prevent words like AGGĔR a *mound* from being pronounced like *anger.*

244. G has a proper character in Sanscrit, as in the original of the Latin word CŌNChX a *conk shell,* and its Greek form, in which it is represented by the gamma. It is also found in the original of ANGUSTUS *narrow,* from the Sanscrit verb AGG to *contract.*

245. G was in some cases derived from M by assimilation, as in PRINCEPS (PRIMICEPS), SĬNCĬPŭT (SEMICAPUT), HORUNCE (HORUMCE) ŪNQVXM (UMQVAM).

246. In transcribing Roman words, the Greeks used their gamma instead of [N] when this character represented *ng*, as in the name of the British tribe CANGÏANI, which became ΚΑΓΚΑΝὄΙ in Greek, as Plutarch uses ΠΡΙΓΚΙΠΙΑ for PRĪNCĪPÏA; affording additional proof of the guttural nature of the Latin sound. ·

G

247. G (*gay*) is heard in the English words *gear, give, gay, get, go.* It is the sonant of *Cay*, and was represented by the same character until the little mark was added which distinguishes [G] from [C]. This mark was introduced by Carvilius, after whom it may be named a *carvilium*.

248. At a remote period, the CELTAE or Kelts entered Spain from France by crossing the Pyrenees, and having become permanently established, they formed with the Iberians the CELTI-BERI.

. 249. This accounts for the Keltic names in Spain which the Romans adopted; and for the occurrence of the same names in Spain and England, as *Abono* in the former and *Avon* in the latter; or that of *Jura* in the Hebrides, and in Switzerland. *Asturias* is derived from AS a *torrent* and TIR *land*, meaning *the land of torrents; Sardinia* from SARD *the larger*, and INIS *island;* and *Lusitania* from TANA *the country*, O *of*, LUIS *flowers.**

250. The languages of the Keltic stock, having preserved the Roman gay and cay pure to the present day, supply us with the pronunciation of ancient Latinized names, as TULINGI from TUL a *flood;* UNGEAD, *leaping;* CINGETORIX from CINGEAD *valiant,* and RIG (Latin REGS) a *king;* COGIDUNUS from COGAC *war,* and DUN a *hill;* VERGESILAÝNUS from FEAR (Latin VIR) a *man;* GALS *expert,* SAELAN (with a) *spear.* The name of a British king, VORTIGERN, is from FOR, *chief,* and TIGERNA, *lord;* and that of the British tribe DUROTRIGES is from DUR, *water,* and TRIG, an *inhabitant.*

251. In French, *Guines* is derived from GISNA; and *Bigorre*

* The Gael and Cymbri, by Sir W. Betham, Dublin, 1834. The works of Johnes and of Prichard may be consulted on the same subject.

5

from BIGERRENSIS AGER; whilst the German name *Bregentz* is
from BREGENTIUM. In German, Spanish, and some other languages, the character [G] never becomes the representative of a
palatal articulation.

C

252. The Latin [C] cay has the power of [K], and no other;
as in CALCO to *tread*, CALCĬTRO to *kick*, CALCĔŬS a *sandal*. The
character [⟨] was used at an early period as the representative
both of G and C, whilst [C] has the third place in the Roman
alphabet, which is occupied by [Γ] gamma in Greek.

253. In the name GAJUS or CAJUS the sonant or surd form is
used indifferently, and the Sanscrit JUG (*yoog*) to *throw*, produced
the Latin JĀCĬO. In the double form TRĪCĒSĬMŬS *thirtieth* and
TRIGESIMUS, if [C] represents s, [G] represents English *z*; or if
the latter represents *dzhi*, the former represents *tshi*, as in Italian.

254. "The uniformity of pronunciation in C, G, &c., when followed by a vowel, is strikingly confirmed by the silence of all
the ancient critics and grammarians, who, though treating expressly of pronunciation, never indicate any variety."—*G. Walker*
in *Scheller.* This argument is strengthened by the fact that the
ancients are sufficiently explicit upon the varying power of [N]
and [M].

255. In the following lists the words written in the first column
are derived from those of the second, and it will be remembered
(§ 17) that palatals do not change to gutturals.

SANCTUM	SANCITUM
DOCTUM	DOCITUM
LECTUM	LECITUM
VINCTUM	VINCITUM
DECURIA	DECEM
CEPĪ	CĂPĬO
PARCI	PARCUS
SĒCIUS	SĔCUS
AUDĀCTĔR	AUDĀCĬTĔR
ALLECTO	ALLICIO
ŏCĒLLŬS	ŏCŭLŭS

256. The organic change from C to S was indicated in Latin orthography, as in CĒNSĔO and SĒNTĬO *to be of opinion;* CĒNSŬS *the censor's valuation,* SĒNSŬS *sense* (from the same root); FUL-CRUM a *prop,* FULCIO I *prop,* FULSI I *have propped.* We find also RAV̇CIO, RAV̇SI; and SARCIO, SARSI; which, as variations respectively of the same word, would have been written similarly if so pronounced.

257. [K] is used in writing the Greek form of CAĖDO to *strike* or *kill,* which is the Gothic *scathia* and English *scath.* Yet CAĖDO is frequently read as if it were SĪDO to *perch,* or CĒDO to *grant.* Moreover, the same root gives rise to CEDO and CADO to *fall* (§ 55), whence OCCASUS a *fall, death,* and ōCCĬDO to *perish.* LŪCĔRNĂ a *lantern* became LUKARN in Gothic, and *leuchte* in German; and the Gothic FASKJA is from the Latin FASCĬĂ a *band.*

258. The guttural contact in ĀCĔR or ĀCRĬS *sharp, bold,* is preserved in *acrid* and *eager;* and in MĂCĔR and the English *meagre,* the French *maigre,* and the German *mager.* It is also preserved in the Irish CĒR, in Latin CERA, *wax;* *airgiott,* Latin ĀRGĒNTŭM, *silver;* CĔL, Latin CĒLO, to *conceal.*

259. The Greek KYKNŎS a *swan,* is the Latin CȲCNŬS or CȲGNŬS, and the modern Persian QUQNUS; a *cherry* is KIRAS in Arabic, CĔRĂSŬS in Latin, and *kirsche* in German; and the Greek MĒKAO to *bleat,* became the Latin MICEO, the German *meckeren,* and the Lithuanian *mikenu.*

260. If the initial of the Latin word CĬThĂRĂ (spelt with K in Greek) was a palatal, the Italian *chitarra* (*ch* as *k*), French *guitare,* and English *guitar* would have a doubtful etymology, and the same doubt would exist in the case of the German words *keller* a *cellar,* *kerker* a *prison,* *kicher* a *chickpea,* which are from the Latin CĔLLĂRIUM, CĂRCĔR, CĬCĔR; or with the English words *elk* from ALCES, and *skink* from SCINCUS, a *kind of lizard.*

261. The Sanscrit SCHAL (H pure after K) to *swerve,* gave rise to the Greek SKŎLŎS, whence the Latin SCĒLŭS *guilt,* and subse-quently the Gothic SKULA, and modern Westphalian s'chULD; so that [ꞩC] in Latin is not a double character for S, any more

than *septic*, *sin* are identical in English with *sceptic* and *skin* (properly *scin*, from the Anglo-saxon).

262. The following Keltic etymologies of Latin names from Betham (§ 249), show the guttural nature of Latin Cay (§ 15). CALLAICI, from CAOILEACH, *narrow* (the narrow slip); AVLERCI, from ALL *great*, and LEARG *plain;* CERONES, from CAOR *sheep;* ICENI, from GAN *bounds*, and OICE the *sea*.

263. The consonant cay has been preserved in the modern names following:—

Kaiserlautern	from	CAESAREA AD LUTRAM.
Kaiserswerd	"	CAESARIS VERDA.
Kylbourg	"	CELBIS BURGUS.
Querquinez (qu=k)	"	CERCINA.
Draguinan	"	DRACENUM.
Exilles	"	OCELUM.
Selefkeh	"	SELEUCIA.

The following Syrian names are from the maps of the Society for the Diffusion of Useful Knowledge:—

Ladikíyeh	from	LAODICEA.
Kaisáríyeh	"	CAESAREA.
Killis	"	CILIZA.
Antakia	"	ANTIOCHIA.
Kerak	"	CHARAX.

The following words are from a vocabulary of *Albanian* given in Diefenbach's work.* *Ch* has the power of *k*.

Fachie	from	FACIES.
Pache	"	PACE.
Pische	"	PISCIS
Kepä	"	CEPAE.
Sckanduem	"	SCINTILLA.

264. When a prefix is added to a Latin word whose initial consonant is different from the final of the prefix, an adapting change called *assimilation* usually takes place in the prefix.

265. Thus AD *to* becomes AN when a prefix to NECTO to *bind,*

---

* Ueber die jetzigen romanischen Schriftsprachen, u. s. w. Leipzig, 1831.

forming ANNECTO to *connect*. The same prefix is modified in the first syllable of the compounds ALLATRO to *bark at*, ATTRĬBŬO to *attribute*, APPELLO to *drive towards*, AFFLŬO to *flow towards*, ARRŎGO to *claim*, ASSĪDEO to *sit at*; whilst in ADDUCO it remains pure. In PŌMŌĔRĬŬM a *limit*, POST is reduced to PO.

266. AD becomes AC by assimilation before cay, as in ACCŎLO to *dwell near*, ACCEPTŬS *accepted*, ACCĪNGO to *gird;* and AG before *gay*, as in AGGRĂVO to *aggravate;* AGGĔRO to *heap together*. Priscian cites QVICQVAM (from QVIDQVAM) and ACCIDIT, as instances of this change from *day* to *cay*. All these examples prove that the conjoined letters had the same sound, and to pronounce them differently reverses the Latin practice.

267. When a consonant character is doubled to represent assimilations, both should be pronounced.

268. The operation of assimilation is seen in the change of N to *ng* (§§ 242, 246) in words used as examples of the change *by the ancients themselves*, as ANGĔLŬS, ĬNGĔŭŬS, LŌNGĪNŬS; and no exceptions are adduced to this change before Cay and Gay preceding I and E, so that they must each have been uniform in all cases; for had they been palatalized in ANCĪLLA and LŌNGĪ-Nŭs, the N preceding them would necessarily have remained pure.

269. Every one pronounces the second C in ECCU^m *behold him* like the first, yet this word being a contraction of ECCĔ ĪLLŭM, if a sibilant is placed in ECCE, it should have a place in the derivative. So from HĪC *here* are formed HICCE *this*, and HĪCCĬNĔ *he*.

*270. The Greek character [K] was never properly naturalized in Latin, nor was it used as in the modern Teutonic languages, where cay would be likely to become s; but (according to the author of "Living Latin") to prevent *cay* from becoming *gay;* and as this distinction took place only before the single vowel A, and was obviated by a difference of character, the [K] became useless, and was so considered by Priscian, who says it has no other value than [C]. Varro and Nigidius Figulus (§ 292) rejected the character K, whilst Quintilian, Terentian and others considered it useless.

271. According to Gregorius Placentinus [K] at one time had

a syllabic power equivalent to CA, when CARŭS was written [KRUS] but read CARUS.

272. For the sake of brevity, the Romans introduced into their numerous inscriptions a multitude of abbreviations, in which a few initial characters, or a single one, represent an entire word; as [C. CL. R.] for CAVSA CLARI REGI.

273. Manutius gives a list of fifty words for which the character [C] stands; thirty for [Q], and twelve for [K]. Among the last are CXLENDAE, CXRŭS, CXPŭT, CXLŭMNĬX, words sometimes spelt with [K], a practice which the inscriptions fostered, although they were intended merely to prevent confusion by assisting the memory in reading them.

274. In reading Latin words as if they were represented by English characters, there is a singular discrepancy in the case of [C, G], which have preserved their pure power before A when the character is insulated, but not before [I] when incorrectly read AJ, nor before AE, as in CAĖNEPOLIS (the modern Qené or Keneh) although in ancient inscriptions [K] is sometimes found in the latter case, as in KAĖSONIA, KAĖSĭŭs.

275. If C and G had not their pure power before I E, as in *gear, gay, key, cane*, the alphabet could not represent these syllables, and Latin would be a more corrupt language than any of those derived from it, and, in fact, the most anomalous known.

*276. The ready interchange of C and G, &c., seems to prove that the surds P, T, C, were what Rapp terms "indifferent," or pronounced with a greater surface of the organs in contact, as in some modern languages; a phenomenon which causes surd and sonant to be confounded, as in German, where *dinte* or *tinte* (ink), *brod* or *brot* (bread), are used according to the inclination of the speaker.

277. C and G must be fully pronounced before N (§ 19), as in the German word *gneiss* (GNAJS) *a kind of rock; knie* (the old English *knee*); and in the Irish *cnáib*, Latin CXNNXBĬS *hemp; gne*, Latin GĖNŭS KĬNd. The same remark applies to T in TMOLŭS, the name of a mountain; and to P in the proper name PTŎLĖMAĖŭS, and in PSXLMUS (PSALM in German and Flemish, and SALM in Danish). The Greek combination KT is found in

Latin in borrowed proper names like CTESIAS, and although it is somewhat difficult, it must be pronounced if accuracy is desired, as in some of the aboriginal languages of America.

X

278. According to Maximus Victorinus and Diomedes, "the ancients," before the invention of [x], wrote GS and CS, the former in words inflected with G, like REX, REXI, MAXIMUS, ĀNXĬŪS, and the latter in such as are inflected with C, as PIX, LUX, FELIX, DIXI. In cases of doubt, as in NIX (compare NINGO), CONNIXI, ALEXANDER, [x] may be read CS, especially as Varro (a cotemporary of Cicero) asserts that no one can distinguish any difference between its two powers.

Ch

279. Chi is the aspirate of C, a sound which is retained in modern Greek, Scotch, German, Spanish, and many other European languages.

280. In Latin, chi occurs in words taken directly from the Greek, and when it cannot be pronounced, it may be replaced with C, as in the Latin double forms ChARITAS *charity*, COChLEA a *snail*, and (more correctly) CĀRĬTĀS, CŌCLĒX. The pronunciation should, however, follow the orthography. § 19.

281. The Greek chi sometimes became G in Latin, as in GALBANUM, ANGO, LINGO, CULIGNA; and H, as in HUMOR, HERES, HIEMS, HIO, HIRUNDO; but more frequently C as in ORCA, LANCEA, SCINDO.

282. In old Latin the Greek chi was replaced by Cay, as in the inscriptive forms BRACIO, BACAS (BACChAS), BACANALIBUS, ANTIOCO (ANTIOCO̦), subsequently pronounced ANTIOChU̱ by the Greek scholars, who were numerous in Rome. So the proper names ChLOE and ChARMOSYNE were Latinized at an early period into CLOE and CARMOSNE.

CH

*283. C followed by H (§ 194) is found in the Latin words CHORS (from COHORS), PULCHER (also sculptured PULCER), AN-

between Latin and Armenian wrtg, this rule will prevent Armenians from reading Latin at al although they learn it.

English analogies will allow a pyrc to be read as a tribrachys *pro in hesitation or hesitation*, is to annexed foot note*), and a fully pronounced dissyllable to be used as a monosyllable, as *flower, flower, lower, less's*, &c. T quotation will show whether it is correct to say that "In Enlish heroic verse, every line consists of ten syllables, five short al five long."

Quantity being a matter of the nice, the varieties of Latin metre first must be judged by the e (so at least thought Horace and Cicero), that being a lon syllable which is long in pronunciation. Hence in English rding, the feet in HŎMĬNĬBŬS and different are identical, because both are pronounced in the same time, instead of the twoirst syllables of the latter carrying the entire time of the forer word. It is chiefly inattention to quantity which annoys the student when he is learning to distinguish a proceleusmaticus on a dispondens or a dijambus, or to determine whether the stare of ARMĬMĔNTĀRĬŬM is molossidactylic or dispondeutiprhic, to be of no use to him when known, if he makes it antiochiodactylic, by reading according to false quantity; especially if his Hudibrastic teacher is satisfied with unpolysllllabicalljical names of the feet, rather than with the feet themselves.†

---

* In the following example to is saned short, whilst *too* or *two* would be brought and *throng* is short when counted with *wrong*. The succession of short syllables in the first line, and long ones in the second, conveys the idea of a rout followed by pursuit appears when the battle begins. The first is rapid, and the second diverse, so that *and* and *men* might have been marked as long.

| | | fight tht thick bat- | tālĭŏns | thrŏng, |
| Shields step'd to | shields tnd mēn drōve | mĕn ĭ- | lŏng. |

Pope's Homer's Iliad, iv. 485.

† If had tried words tiy to show why
And tell what rhimes did it by;
For his a ridiculoust...
Teach nothing his nice Hic ...

Hudibras, i. 85—90.

English poetry is written and read appreciatingly without a knowledge of the Lati feet, with which some have attempted to cripple it. As Latin f t depend upon *quantity*, and English feet upon *accent*, the two c not have the same names. In English there is no difference i the use of what would be a molossus in Latin, as lōathesōmenē ; an antibacchius, as flāmīnglў; a dactyl, as hārmŏnў; and a tr achys, as pĭtĭfŭl; one being capable of replacing the other if e proper accent be preserved, as *pĭtĭfŭl ĕnĕmĭes* instead of the 7o first feet in the following approxima- tion to an English sca ional hexameter, compared with one of Virgil's: but although iis may be done, the iambus bíllōw can- not replace the iambus lòw.*

"ĀRMX   VĬ-|RŪ^mQVĔ -|NŌ TRŌJ|Æ   QVĪ|PRĪMŬS XB|ŌRĪS."
ārms ănd thĕ|hērŏ |sīng whō|first frōm| ĭlĭŏn's |bōrdĕrs.

Literary people fanc; hat—

"Frōm thĕ lŏw | p ısŭres ŏf | thĭs făllĕn | nātŭre..."

is an example of dact c verse, although *low* is as long as the next syllable; *this* is sl ter than *fall;* and the first syllable of iature is as short as th second, or equivalent to *fate,* which is s short as *fat,* and shc er than *fane.* This example, like my vn, has the natural oi rose accent at the beginning of each)t, which is not the se in Latin. The following line will erefore give the uncla al reader a better idea of Latin versifi- tion, in which it may ıppen that a foot (like the fourth) is thout a natural accent This accent is marked in the example, e long with a grave ac itual, and the short with an acute one. rĕās is given as an Er ish word.

tòrms ănd bíl|lōws ănd ɔr|rōrs thrèe|fŏld thrō|Bòrĕăs'|wàilĭngs.

This is prose, and if ıtin verse was recited with the prose nt (and the Italians ecite it in this manner), the listener) d not distinguish it ɔm prose, except by the quantity, and

---

* Thĕ | bĭllōws | fl ; ĭn   : ōrdĕr | tŏ thĕ | shōre,
  Thĕ | wāve bĕ- | h l rōlls , ōn thĕ | wāve bĕ- | fōre.
                                Pope's Homer's Iliad, iv. 480.

CHORA (but Marius Victorinus considered ANCORA the more cr-
rect word) and LACHRIMA, which seems to be less proper tha
LACRIMA. The following forms are taken from three differet
inscriptions, a line from each :

MISER . QVID . GEMIS . ET . LACRIMAS

IGITVR . LE'CTOR . LACHRIMES

TRIB . LACRVMAS . POS

284. Plutarch introduces chi into the Greek form (Πнλχɛϛ) (
the name PULCHER, following a Greek rule (note 211), or mi:
taking every union of c and H for the Greek chi.   The sam
thing occurs in the Greek form of GRACCHUS or GRACCUS, fron
which [H] is rejected by Varro and some inscriptions.

285. The power of c and H is doubtful in Punic proper name.
like BARCHA, BOCCHUS.

---

9. GLOTTAL CONSONANTS.

Q

286. The Oriental Qof and Greek qoppa (Ϙ) is a very ancient
character; its form in Egyptian hieroglyphic writing is the figure
of a man's head and neck, the latter being for some time represented by a vertical line (as in the Greek ϙΡΟΤΩΝ for KRŎTǪN;
ϙΟΡΙΝΘΟ$, &c., upon old coins), which degenerated into the
ordinary appendage.   In Hebrew and Samaritan, which are written from right to left, the tail is placed upon the left side.

287. The sound, a glottal K, was found in Hebrew, Phenician,
and Zend; and exists in Hindoostàni, Arabic, Persian, Coptic,
Armenian, and Gurgistanic (Georgian).   It was not a Latin
sound, although it was probably found in Italy, judging from
Etruscan monuments.   Modern scholars use [Q] to represent this
sound.

288. If Qof had been a Roman consonant, it would be represented in certain words of Eastern origin, as CŎRNŭ a *horn* (Hebrew and Arabic QARN); QORBAN a *gift*, a Hebrew word introduced
by Saint Mark vii. 11; CĂMĪNŭS a *furnace* (Arabic QAMIN, Per-

sian QUMIN a *chimney*); CXRXBUS a *crab*; (Arabic XQRAB a *scorpion*); CYMATIUM *wavy* carved work, from the Greek KYMA a *wave*, and Hebrew QUM to *rise*. To these probably belong CXTŭs, Arabic *qitth* a *cat*; and VICIX a *vetch*; Greek BIKION, Arabic BAQL. §§ 168, 172, 175.

289. In the following proper names, qof and not cay occurs in the originals: DAMASQUS, ISAₐQ, JAQOB, QXĬN, QEMŭEL, XMₐLèQ (ₐ as in *fall*), AQₑLDÀMA, *Acts* i. 19.

*290. The use of [Q] in Latin was to indicate that the following [V] represented a consonant, but it became as useless as K when the two forms [V, U,] were introduced, so that its use should have been relinquished, as in the ancient examples ACVAE for AQVAE, CVO for QVO, and CVANDO for QVANDO. The last word is retained in the Spanish *cuando*.

291. The character COO was of little account in indicating the consonant V, because the difficulty was not obviated in cases like ŪNGVENTŭ^m an *unguent*, SXNGVĬS *blood*, SVXDEO to *persuade*, so that regularity in orthography as well as ancient authority would allow it to be rejected.

292. On account of its identity with C in Latin, some ancient authors did not consider COO a letter, and Vellius Longus states that QVIS might be written CVIS. The celebrated orator and friend of Cicero, Licinius Calvus, avoided this character, and Nigidius Figulus made no use of K, Q, nor X.

293. In a few ancient examples [U] followed [Q] as the representative of a vowel, as in LAQUS, QURA, QURVUS, PEQUNIA; for LACUS, etc. It would have been etymological in XBXQŭs and SYQXMŌRUS.

H

294. H is the liquid of the glottal contact, in which the requisite amount of interruption is secured by emitting the unvocalized breath with a certain velocity, and not by reducing the vocal passage. It is heard in the English and German syllables *hut*, *hat*, *held*.

295. This sound has become almost entirely obsolete in the Romish languages, which might lead us to believe that it did not

CHORA (but Marius Victorinus considered ANCORA the more correct word) and LACHRIMA, which seems to be less proper than LACRIMA. The following forms are taken from three different inscriptions, a line from each:

MISER . QVID . GEMIS . ET . LACRIMAS

IGITVR . LE'CTOR . LACHRIMES

TRIB . LACRVMAS . POS

284. Plutarch introduces chi into the Greek form (Πυλχες) of the name PULCHER, following a Greek rule (note 211), or mistaking every union of C and H for. the Greek chi. The same thing occurs in the Greek form of GRACCHUS or GRACCUS, from which [H] is rejected by Varro and some inscriptions.

285. The power of C and H is doubtful in Punic proper names like BARCHA, BOCCHUS.

---

9. GLOTTAL CONSONANTS.

Q

286. The Oriental Qof and Greek qoppa (ϙ) is a very ancient character; its form in Egyptian hieroglyphic writing is the figure of a man's head and neck, the latter being for some time represented by a vertical line (as in the Greek ϙΡΟΤΩΝ for KRŎTŎN; ϙΟΡΙΝΘΟΣ, &c., upon old coins), which degenerated into the ordinary appendage. In Hebrew and Samaritan, which are written from right to left, the tail is placed upon the left side.

287. The sound, a glottal K, was found in Hebrew, Phenician, and Zend; and exists in Hindoostàni, Arabic, Persian, Coptic, Armenian, and Gurgistanic (Georgian). It was not a Latin sound, although it was probably found in Italy, judging from Etruscan monuments. Modern scholars use [Q] to represent this sound.

288. If Qof had been a Roman consonant, it would be represented in certain words of Eastern origin, as CŎRNŬ a *horn* (Hebrew and Arabic QARN); QORBAN a *gift*, a Hebrew word introduced by Saint Mark vii. 11; CXMĬNŬS a *furnace* (Arabic QAMIN, Per-

sian QUMIN a *chimney*); CXRXBUS a *crab*; (Arabic XQRAB a *scorpion*); CYMXTIUM *wavy* carved work, from the Greek KYMA a *wave*, and Hebrew QUM to *rise*. To these probably belong CXTŭS, Arabic *qitth* a *cat;* and VĬCĬX a *vetch;* Greek BIKION, Arabic BAQL. §§ 168, 172, 175.

289. In the following proper names, qof and not cay occurs in the originals: DAMASQUS, ISAA̯Q, JAQOB̈, QXĪN, QĔMŪEL, XMA̯LèQ (A̯ as in *fall*), AQɛLDàMA, *Acts* i. 19.

*290. The use of [Q] in Latin was to indicate that the following [V] represented a consonant, but it became as useless as K when the two forms [V, U,] were introduced, so that its use should have been relinquished, as in the ancient examples ACVAE for AQVAE, CVO for QVO, and CVANDO for QVANDO. The last word is retained in the Spanish *cuando*.

291. The character COO was of little account in indicating the consonant V, because the difficulty was not obviated in cases like ŪNGVĔNTŪᵐ an *unguent*, SXNGVĬS *blood*, SVADĔO to *persuade*, so that regularity in orthography as well as ancient authority would allow it to be rejected.

292. On account of its identity with C in Latin, some ancient authors did not consider COO a letter, and Vellius Longus states that QVIS might be written CVIS. The celebrated orator and friend of Cicero, Licinius Calvus, avoided this character, and Nigidius Figulus made no use of K, Q, nor X.

293. In a few ancient examples [U] followed [Q] as the representative of a vowel, as in LAQUS, QURA, QURVUS, PEQUNIA; for LACUS, etc. It would have been etymological in XBXQŭS and SYQXMŌRUS.

H

294. H is the liquid of the glottal contact, in which the requisite amount of interruption is secured by emitting the unvocalized breath with a certain velocity, and not by reducing the vocal passage. It is heard in the English and German syllables *hut*, *hat*, *held*.

295. This sound has become almost entirely obsolete in the Romish languages, which might lead us to believe that it did not

ANCORA (but Marius Victorinus considered ANCORA the more correct word) and LACHRIMA, which seems to be less proper than LACRIMA. The following forms are taken from three different inscriptions, a line from each:

MISER . QVID . GEMIS . ET . LACRIMAS
IGITVR . LECTOR . LACHRIMES
TRIB . LACRYMAS . POS.

284. Plutarch introduces chi into the Greek form (Πωχις) of the same PVLCHER, following a Greek rule (note 211), or mistaking every union of C and H for the Greek chi. The same thing occurs in the Greek form of GRACCHUS or GRACCUS, from which [H] is rejected by Varro and some inscriptions.

285. The power of C and H is doubtful in Punic proper names like MARCHA, BOCCHUS.

———

b. GLOTTAL CONSONANTS.

Q

286. The Oriental qof and Greek qoppa (Ϙ) is a very ancient character; its form in Egyptian hieroglyphic writing is the figure of a man's head and neck, the latter being for some time represented by a vertical line (as in the Greek ϘΡΟΤΩΝ for KROTON; ϘΥΡΗΝΗ, &c., upon old coins), which degenerated into the binary appendage. In Hebrew and Samaritan, which are written from right to left, the tail is placed upon the left side.

287. The sound, a glottal K, was found in Hebrew, Phenician, and Zend; and exists in Hindoostani, Arabic, Persian, Coptic, Russian, and Gurgistanic (Georgian). It was not a Latin sound, although it was probably found in Italy, judging from Etruscan monuments. Modern scholars use [Q] to represent this sound.

288. If qof had been a Roman consonant, it would be used in certain words of Eastern origin, as CORNI... row and Arabic QARN); QORBAN a gift, a Hebrew w... Saint Mark vii. 11; CAMINUS a furnace (Arab...

sian QUMIN a *chimney*); CXRXBUS a *crab*
scorpion); CYMATIUM *wavy* carved work, fr¢
a *wave*, and Hebrew QUM to *rise*. To th
CXTŭs, Arabic *qitth* a *cat;* and VĬCĬX a *ve*
Arabic BAQL. §§ 168, 172, 175.

289. In the following proper names, qo¹
in the originals: DAMASQUS, ISAAQ, JAQ¢
XMALèQ (A as in *fall*), AQɛLDÀMA, *Acts* i. 1⁹

*290. The use of [Q] in Latin was to indi
ing [V] represented a consonant, but it bec
when the two forms [V, U,] were introdu¢
should have been relinquished, as in the anci
for AQVAE, CVO for QVO, and CVANDO for
word is retained in the Spanish *cuando*.

291. The character COO was of little acco1
consonant V, because the difficulty was not o
ūNGVENTūᵐ an *unguent*, SANGVĬS *blood*, s¹
so that regularity in orthography as well ª
would allow it to be rejected.

292. On account of its identity with c in
authors did not consider *coo* a letter, and V
that QVIS might be written CVIS. The e¢
friend of Cicero, Licinius Calvus, avoided
Nigidius Figulus made no use of K, Q, nor x

'293. In a few ancient examples [U] follo¹
sentative of a vowel, as in LAQUS, QURA, QU
LACUS, etc. It would have been etymolog¹
SYQXMŌRUS.

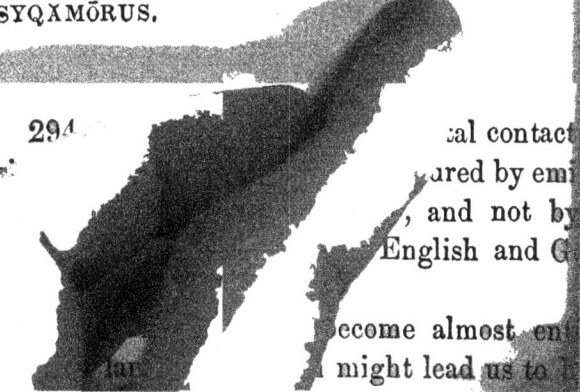

294 ... ;al contact
,.ared by emi
, and not b¹
English and G

ecome almost en
might lead us to

exist in Latin. The ancient authors, however, speak of it as an aspiration, and no exception is made for words like HŎNŎR or HONOS *honor*, HŌRA an *hour*.

296. In ARIŎLATIO or HARIOLATIO, and some other words, H was indifferently used or rejected; whilst AVE *hail!* was esteemed more correct than HAVE.

297. The following are a few of those words likely to be confounded by the French and Italians, whose vernacular has lost the typical aspirate:

ABĪTŬS a *departure*.	HABĪTŬS *condition*.
AC *and*.	HAC *this way*.
AMATOR a *lover*.	HAMATOR a *deceiver*.
ARA an *altar*.	HARA a *hogsty*.
ÉLĬCES *gutters*.	HÉLĬCES *spirals*.
EV! *well done*.	HEV, HAV! *alas*.
ŌSTĬA *doors*.	HŌSTĬA a *victim*.

*298. "There seems no good ground for supposing that the sound of H was ever suppressed by accurate speakers."—*G. Walker.* The rule (§ 19) would require H to be pronounced after a vowel in the interjections OH, PROH; as in the Bohemian word *lehky;* the Konza word for *nose*, which is the English syllable *paw* followed by H, as if *pa'h;* and in the Hebrew words GOMŌRRAH, MILCAH, MACHPELÀH, REBEQAH, LŎTH *Lot*, NĪNĔVEH, EPHAH.

299. H occurs rarely after N, as in ANHELO to *gasp;* and in the proper name PANORMUS, which stands PANHORMUS upon some coins, as SYNHODUS stands for SYNODUS in an inscription.

300. Catullus condemns the affectation of saying HINSIDIAS for INSIDIAS, and CHOMMODA, that is C'HO-MMO-DA, for COMMODA.

NOTES.

Page 5. As examples of the elision of syllables in poetry may be cited MULTUM ILLE ET TERRIS, which is read MULT' ILL' ET TERRIS; ULTRO ASIAM, read ULTR' ASIAM. So we find SCJ'-ABSURDE for SCIO ABSURDE; TV'ARBITRATU for TUO ARBITRATU; M'ERCLE for MEO HERCULE; and MJ'AJC for MEA HAEC. So in Italian poetry we find *bevve* for *bevette; capéi* for *capélli; cor* for *cógliere; dicestu* for *dicesti tu*, &c.

Page 17. According to Adam's so-called "Latin Grammar," Prosody "teaches the *proper* accent and *quantity* of syllables, the *right pronunciation* of words, and the measures of verse.... A long syllable in pronouncing requires double the time of a short one... In most Latin words of one or two syllables, according to *our* manner of pronouncing, we can hardly distinguish by the ear a long syllable from a short one." That is to say, if this author were to hear the word AJAX or ĂJAX, he could not tell whether the speaker used a long or a short initial. It is well that *Prosody* teaches the proper quantity of syllables, because the false grammars do not; the rules just quoted, and all others in the same book, being contradicted, superseded, and rendered worthless by the first paragraph, in which the learner is informed that "Latin *should* be accented and pronounced by us according to the prevailing analogies of our own language, without regard to the prosodial accent and quantity of the ancients." Hence if "our own language" is Italian, SINE DIE contains four syllables and as many vowels; if German, three syllables and vowels; and if English, two syllables (like IN FINE) with a dipthong in each, such being the prevailing analogies; and as these do not exist between Latin and Armenian writing, this rule will prevent Armenians from reading Latin at all, although they learn it.

English analogies will allow a pyrrhyc to be read as a tribrachys (as in bat-*tal-ion* or bat-*tal-i-on*, in the annexed foot note*), and a fully pronounced dissyllable to be used as a monosyllable, as *flour, flower, bower, heav'n,* &c. The quotation will show whether it is correct to say that "In English heroic verse, every line consists of ten syllables, five short and five long."

Quantity being a matter of the voice, the varieties of Latin poetic feet must be judged by the ear (so at least thought Horatius and Cicero), *that* being a long syllable which is long in pronunciation. Hence in English reading, the feet in HŎMĬNĬBŬS and FŌRTĪSSĬMŬS are identical, because both are pronounced in the same time, instead of the two first syllables of the latter occupying the entire time of the former word. It is chiefly inattention to quantity which annoys the student when he is learning to distinguish a proceleusmaticus from a dispondens or a dijambus; or to determine whether the nature of ĀRMĀMĒNTĀRĬŬM is molossidactylic or dispondentipyrrhic, to be of no use to him when known, if he makes it antibacchiodactylic, by reading according to false quantity; especially if his Hudibrastic teacher is satisfied with tragododidascalicological names of the feet, rather than with the feet themselves.†

---

* In the following example *to* is marked short, whilst *too* or *two* would be long; and *throng* is short when compared with *wrong*. The succession of short syllables in the first line, and of long ones in the second, conveys the idea of a rush followed by greater composure when the battle begins. The first is rapid, and the second deliberate, so that *and* and *men* might have been marked as long.

| Sŏ | tŏ thĕ | fīght thĕ | thĭck băt- | tăliŏns | thrŏng, |
| Shĭelds | ūrg'd ōn | shĭelds ănd | mĕn drŏve | mĕn ă- | lōng. |

Pope's Homer's Iliad, iv. 485.

† H' had hàrd words réady to show whỳ
And téll what rùles he did it bỳ;
For àll a rhétorícían's rùles
Teach nóthing bút to nàme his tòols.

Hudibras, i. 85—90.

English poetry is written and read appreciatingly without a knowledge of the Latin feet, with which some have attempted to cripple it. As Latin feet depend upon *quantity*, and English feet upon *accent*, the two cannot have the same names. In English there is no difference in the use of what would be a molossus in Latin, as lōathesōmenēss; an antibacchius, as flāmīnglў; a dactyl, as hārmŏnў; and a tribrachys, as pĭtĭfŭl; one being capable of replacing the other if the proper accent be preserved, as *pĭtĭfŭl ĕnĕmĭes* instead of the two first feet in the following approximation to an English scansional hexameter, compared with one of Virgil's: but although this may be done, the iambus bíllōw cannot replace the iambus bĕlòw.*

"ĀRMĀ VĬ-|RŪᵐQVĔ CX-|NŌ TRŌJ|Æ   QVĪ|PRĪMŬS ĀB|ŌRĪS."
ārms ănd thĕ|hērŏ   ĭ |sĭng whŏ|fĭrst frōm| īlĭŏn's |bōrdērs.

Literary people fancy that—

"Frōm thĕ lŏw | plēasŭres ŏf | thĭs făllĕn | nātŭre..."

is an example of dactylic verse, although *low* is as long as the next syllable; *this* is shorter than *fall;* and the first syllable of *nature* is as short as the second, or equivalent to *fate*, which is as short as *fat*, and shorter than *fane*. This example, like my own, has the natural or prose accent at the beginning of each foot, which is not the case in Latin. The following line will therefore give the unclassical reader a better idea of Latin versification, in which it may happen that a foot (like the fourth) is without a natural accent. This accent is marked in the example, the long with a grave accentual, and the short with an acute one. Bŏrĕās is given as an English word.

Stòrms ănd bíl|lōws ănd hór|rōrs thrèe|fōld thrò|Bòrĕās'|wàilīngs.

This is prose, and if Latin verse was recited with the prose accent (and the Italians recite it in this manner), the listener could not distinguish it from prose, except by the quantity, and

* Thĕ | bĭllōws | flŏat ĭn | ōrdĕr | tŏ thĕ | shōre,
  Thĕ | wāve bĕ- | hīnd rōlls | ōn thĕ | wāve bĕ- | fōre.
  Pope's Homer's Iliad, iv. 480.

for this accent Bentley contends; whilst Mekerchus was in favor of a mode like scanning. The author of "Living Latin" would have dactyls, anapests, trochees, ånd iambics accented on the long syllable; tribrachs, spondees, and pyrrhics to take the accent upon the first syllable among dactyls, &c., and upon the last in iambic or anapestic verse. The ancient grammarians leave this question in doubt, and amidst such conflicting opinions the least objectionable mode seems to be to pay strict attention to quantity, and to avoid the use of accent. § 25.

Dr. Gally, a literary person of the last century, who has many followers at the present day, asserts incorrectly that "No man can read prose or verse according to both accent and quantity. For every accent, if it is anything, must give some stress to the syllable upon which it is placed; and every stress that is laid upon a syllable must give some extent to it, for every elevation of the voice implieth time, and time is quantity." An unlettered person could not have fallen into such an error. In the Latin Grammar of the Rev. P. Bullion, D. D., N. York, 1843, it is stated that "In Ĕnglish ĕvery accĕnted sўllable is lŏng." If these views were correct, there would be no difference in quantity between *tărry* to remain, and *tärry* from *tar*. See paragraph 47.

§ 5. The names at the end of this paragraph are given in the original character to enforce the views of the preceding ones. The first name is *St. Petersburg*, the second *el Medina*, and the third *Canton*.

17 *a*. The tongue being in a manner wedged into the throat, its base has not so free a motion as its apex, so that palatal letters are more easily made than gutturals. I do not assert that exceptions to the rule of change from guttural to palatal do not occur, although I believe that some of the cases that may be cited are more apparent than real.

b. In accordance with a notion that English orthography must be etymological, I have avoided the use of words which seemed to indicate a change from palatal to guttural, as in "nuiSanCe" from noCeRe (§ 220.) I have consequently been compelled to use the original form of hŏrătĭus, and to avoid the English form of praefatĭo, defensĭo, &c. The corrupt use of [c] in English has caused authors whose classical knowledge could not be doubted, to use this character in writing INSESSŌRES (perhaps as an English word) and *supercede*. Noah Webster says that to spell *sigàr* with [s] is a mistake of the grocers. It is evident that the mistake in writing "defence," &c., is grosser.

18*a*. The Sanscrit SAICA5 *irrigation* (whence the Latin sŭccŭs *juice*) is said to be from the Sanscrit (in English letters) *seetsh*, but this is probably rather modern, and it is more probable that both are from a lost form with a final *cay*, because the English palatals *dzh* and *tsh* are so common in Sanscrit as to induce the belief that *cay* and *gay* must have disappeared from many words before they were written.

b. The Sanscrit SNU *to sprinkle* is supposed to have given rise to the Gothic *snaiws* and old English *snow*, &c., yet the Russian *snieg*, the Gaelic *sneachd*, and Irish SNÁchTŏ, have a guttural which must be looked for in some ancient collateral dialect. The Sanscrit root of the Greek AGΩ has the double form AG and (in English letters) *adzh*, of which the former must be the older, and therefore the true root. The initial of the Sanscrit analogue of *cool*, GELO, GELIDUS is English *dzh*, although it was probably GALITA5 at an earlier period. The Latin MALIGNUS is evidently older than the Sanscrit MALINA5, which probably lost a *gay*. The arguments used in this note tend to disprove views like the following: "Perhaps ζ was retained because the original dialectic sound *dsi* passed over, among the Greeks, into *ksi*."—*Buttman's larger Greek Grammar*, by E. Robinson. Andover, 1839.

c. The English words *quack, cuckoo;* with the Latin COAXO, CUCULO, and their Greek forms, cannot be derived from the Sanscrit CATsh (to which they are referred), because this must be a later form of KÁKH to *cry* and to *laugh*, which gave rise to *chuckle, giggle, gaggle, cackle, chicken* (Angl. CICEN), *cheek* (Dutch *kek*), *cough, hiccup;* and probably *cake, coke, cook, citchen*, if the original idea is connected with the noise of cooking.

d. Although the predominance of palatals in Sanscrit where the Greek preserves the gutturals, leads to the conclusion that in certain points the latter is the older form, this need not prevent us from considering AGΩ as a derivative of AG, because the latter probably occurred in languages which preceded the Greek. On the other hand, the absence of Sanscrit words like GALITA5 is a strong argument against its great antiquity under its present form.

21. "AVLAS ANTIQVI DICEBANT, QVAS NOS DIC-IMUS ŌLLAS."—*Festus.*

26. The following extracts are given to show how imperfectly the rudiments of grammar are defined: "Sentences consist of words; words of one or more syllables; syllables of one or more letters. A *letter* is the *mark of a sound.* Letters [marks of sound] are divided into *vowels* and *consonants.* A vowel [mark of a sound] makes a full sound by itself. A consonant [mark of sound] cannot make a perfect sound without a vowel; as b. d."— *Adam's Latin Grammar, with Improvements.* It appears from this that vowels, consonants, and syllables, instead of being parts of human speech, whether written or unwritten, are merely marks, also called letters; and that the consonants b, d, l, m, &c., cannot make a perfect sound, probably because a mark can make no sound, although a human being can, particularly a Sclavonian, who uses entire words without a vowel, as *smrt, srp, krm, drbl. His* speech, however, does not contain "marks of a sound," but the sounds themselves. The next sentence to the last quoted informs us that "A vowel is properly *called* a *simple sound;* and the sounds formed by the concourse of vowels and consonants *articulate sounds.*" Hence, a sound and the mark of a sound are identical. The sections in the same Grammar devoted to the dipthongs and consonants are equally confused and inaccurate, which is unfortunate in a work which defines Latin Grammar to be "the art of *speaking* and writing the Latin language *correctly.*"

28a. For the forms of the Roman script letters, the *Foreign Quarterly Review* for October, 1841, may be consulted.

b. The first character in Roman inscriptions is not larger than the rest, although a large letter was occasionally used, as I for II in DIs. The use of characters of two sizes (unknown in most alphabets except modern Greek and Roman) is seen in the following copies of parts of ancient inscriptions from Manutius.

c. These examples show that the hyphen was not used, and that the only point was a dot separating the words, but which was not used at the end of a line, or where the modern period point would be used.

d. In print, variations in the form of the characters cannot well be represented. The accentual is probably placed after the character to which it belongs, for the convenience of the printer. It was probably placed above in the original inscriptions.

1

MATV′RA . PER . sTYGIA . MORTE . SEQVAR

2

CONIVGI . SVO

·KARISSIMO . ET . SIBI

3

CONIVGI . CARISSI

MAE . B . M . FEC

4

FEC . F . CARISSIMO . PIISSI

MO . ET . SIBI . ET . SVIS

5

SIT . TIBI . TERRA . LEVIS . MVLIER . DIGNI

SSIMA . VITA . QVAEQVE . TVIS

O′LIM . PERFRVERE′RE . BONIS

6

D . M

D . IVNIO . PRIMIGENIO

QVI . VIX . ANN . XXXV

IVNIA . PALLAS . FECIT

CONIVGI . KARISSIMO

ET . PIENTISSIMO

DE . SE . BENEMERENTI

CVM . QVO . VIXIT . ANNIS

XV . MENSES . VI

DVLCITER . SINE . QVERELLA

32. In Bullion's Latin Grammar, it is stated that "The Latin alphabet consists of 25 letters, the same in name and form as the English, but without the *w.*" The same author discusses the *letters* under one head and the *vowels* under another, and under

the latter we are told that "A *vowel* is a *letter*, which represents a simple sound."

36*a*. Being founded upon organic laws, this table may be made a useful element in the construction of Grammars; and it will be found a more important aid in etymology than any system of false orthography. This will appear in tracing the following words:—

Greek	D	A	K	R	Y	M	A		Latin	P O R C U S		
Latin	L	A	C	R	I	M	A		Germ.	F E R K e L		
Gothic	T	A	G	R					Welsh	P ε R ch i Lh		
French	L	A		R		M	e		Dutch	B i G		
Anglosaxon	T e	A		R					Eng.	P i G		
English	T	I		R					French	P O R C		
Welsh	D a	I	G y R						Irish	M ŭ C		
"	D	U		R, *water.*					Gaelic	M ŭ ch		

The German *p i ch e n* to *ti*pple (or *to*pe), and

p e g e ln to *di*p into (*dive*), give

the English *p i ck e l* a *steep*ing liquid,

the Scotch *p i gg i n* a *di*pping vessel,

the German *b e ck e n* whence *basin* (*pitcher?*), and

the English *m u g.** Compare *Margaret* and *Peggy*.

b. The Roman V (English *w*) is aspirated in the English word *when* (wh-w-e-n), L and R in Welsh, J (English *y*) in Cherokee, and in the English syllable H*ugh*, *hue* or *hew* (yh-y-u). The aspirate of D is heard in *this*, and of G in Dutch, and sometimes in German.

39. Prof. Anthon, in his edition of Zumpt's Latin Grammar, considers the short *e* in *mete long*, and a Professor of Latin and Greek has expressed to me his doubts as to whether the last syllable of *deceit* is any shorter than that of *marine, redeem*, &c. The former, as I pronounce it, is *one fourth of a second* long, and the latter is not less than *half a second*. Any musician who is an accurate timist may decide between us. This view of a short vowel was published by me in a review in 1846.

45. The Italians, whilst they give the same quantity to VĪTTA and VĪTA, give a distinct pronunciation to each consonant indi-

---

* MUG—"I know not whence derived."—*Webster.*

cated in the former, so that the two are perfectly distinguishable in pronunciation.

47. The French (and some other nations) have introduced a corruption in using the accent marks to indicate distinction in sounds, as between *de* and *dé*.

48. These rules for the accent of prose are those of Quintilian, who says besides that a final syllable is not accented. Subsequent grammarians, however, cite exceptions, which Scaliger thought unworthy of attention. Nevertheless, when an author or editor places an accentual in writing RECTÈ, MALÈ, PENNâ, it is to be understood that he wishes these words to be accented accordingly. In my work on the *Freshwater univalve mollusca* of the United States, Philad., 1842, and Monograph of the genus *Leptoxis* (in Chenu's *Illustrations Conchyologiques*), Paris, 1847, I have used accentuals in the Latin descriptions; but in the later CRYPTO-CEPHALINARUM BOREALI-AMERICAE DIAGNOSES CUM SPECIEBUS NOVIS, etc., I have made no use of them, nor of the combined [Æ, Œ], and I have conformed to the European practice of writing adjectives like PENSILVANICUS with a small initial. In deference to the journal in which the latter was published, it is printed in the European character, a Latin character being used at the beginning of a sentence, although in Latin typography in the European character, a small initial may be used after a full point, as practiced by Lipsius, and to some extent in German.

58*a*. Although this is not the place to treat of Greek pronunciation, I may be allowed to give a few words upon the *eta* (H), which I believe to have been the pure Roman E in *vein*. From the formation of this vowel it is more closely allied to A than I is (the latter of which the modern Greeks consider *eta* to have been), and in allied dialects it would be more likely to change with A than if it were identical with I. We accordingly find *eta* in the Ionic words hELIOS, AThENAI, thĒSEUS, sophIE, thorĒCS, &c., and A in hALIOS, AThANAI, thASEUS, sophIA, thorACS, in Doric. The Attic in the three first agrees with the Ionic, and in the two remaining ones with the Doric. So we find λαξεςθαι and ληξεςθαι, from λαγχανω. Compare αϱα, αϱη; αις, ης; λιμην, λιμενος; ποιεω, ποιησω; κῆϛ for κεαϛ, αϛκηϑης or αϛκεϑης, to show that η had a strong relation to ε and α, so that it could not be identical with ι. Cratinus says the cry of the sheep is Βη.

b. The old Doric form GA (the earth) became GE in normal Greek, and this has become GI (or JI) in the modern pronunciation, by the closing of the organs, just as the Latin CLARUS (German *klar*) became *claire* in French and *clear* in English.

69. O LONGUM AVTEM PRODUCTIS LABIIS, RICTU TERETI, etc. —*Victorinus.*

73. U .... ORE CONSTRICTO LABRISQVE PROMINULIS EXHIBETER.—*Capella.*

80. Y ...... APPRESSIS LABRIS SPIRITUQVE PROCEDIT.— *Capella.*

83. That the Greeks represented U by ου or 8 is proved by their orthography of Roman names, as TIBUR Τιβ8ρα, REGULUS, Ρηγ8λος; ALBULA, Αλβ8λα; NOVUMCOMUM, Νοβ8μχομ8μ; VALÉRIA, 8αλεξίας. The following are Greek versions of Latin names in Britain: Σελγουαι SELGOVAE; Νουανται NOVANTAE; Δη8ανα DEVANA; 8ιχτοξια VICTORIA; 8αχομαγοι VACOMAGI; Καξνανιοι CARNABII; 8εν̃τα VENTA; 'Ρ8τ8πιαι RHUTUPIS; Δ8ξοτξιγες DUROTRIGES. The English often pronounce U as *you* and 8 as in round! whilst an English scholar, as if to impress this barbarism permanently upon the Greek, uses 8 for the dipthong in *round*, in his phonetic English alphabet.

96. HEJC occurs in the following vertical inscription (*Manutius*, p. 113. *Aldus*, Venetiis, 1566):—

O	S
S	I
S	T
A	A
H	S
E	U
I	N
C	T

101. "M OBSCURUM IN EXTREMITATE DICTIONUM SONAT, UT TEMPLUM; APERTUM IN PRINCIPIO, UT MAGNUS; MEDIOCRE IN MEDIIS, UT UMBRA."—*Priscian.*

110*a.* "DIPHTHONGI AVTEM DICUNTUR, QVOD BINOS PHTHON-

GOS, HOC EST, VOCES COMPREHENDUNT. NAM SINGULAE VOCÁLES SUAS VOCES HABENT."—*Priscianus*, lib. i.

b. An *inverse* dipthong is where the coalescent precedes the vowel, as in the French words *oie, trois.* This peculiarity is confined almost entirely to the French language, which wants the ordinary or *direct* dipthongs.

111. A dipthong is etymologically and practically a double *sound*, and has nothing to do with the number of characters used in representing it. Yet the French continually speak of words like their *au, eu,* being dipthongs. The English word *aisle* is composed of one dipthong and one consonant, and *ail* of a vowel and a consonant. The Abbé Sicard is in error in saying that *eau* is a word composed of vowels, because *eau (au or ô)* comprehends but a single vowel or continuous voice. In the Spelling-book of Wm. D. Swan, the word *beat* is said to contain a diphthong.

117*a.* I have noticed the peculiarity in the NXDACŏ language of Texas, of the Latin dipthong AV being co-existent with the dissyllabic AU.

b. This distinction is rarely recognized by grammarians. Since the text was printed, I have heard the dipthong OJ in Portuguese, as in ŏJTŏ (in Latin characters) *eight.*

130. "ALPHA SEMPER ATQVE IOTA QVEM PARANT GRAECIS SONI, A ET E NOBIS MINISTRANT."—*Terentianus Maurus.* "IN LATINO RURE HEDUS, QVOD IN URBE, UT IN MULTIS, A ADDITO HAEDUS."—*Varro.*

148*a.* V, LITTERAM QVOTIES ENUNCIAMUS, PRODUCTIS ET COËUNTIBUS LABRIS EFFERIMUS.—*Victorinus Afer.*

b. "The Umbrians and Oscans distinguished between U and V. The latter was a consonant, and was pronounced like our *w.*" "V must have corresponded to our English W."—*Donaldson's Varronianus.*

150*a.* The following strange argument has been adduced to prove that English and French *v* existed in Latin. "The Latin ear was certainly too delicate ever to have suffered the pronunciation *Wox Wentus* instead of *ventus,* which it seems to me would have been as strange to them as *Woice* for *Voice, Went* for *Vent,*

Winegar for *Vinegar,* do to a well-bred person now in England."
—*H. Bonnycastle, Classical Museum,* No. 23.

b. It seems from this that *v* is more of a well-bred sound than *w,* so that of the two words from the same root, *wine* and *vinegar,* the former would be the more vulgar; and that the Germans who acquire English *v* sooner than *w,* throw a "well-bred" and classical air around their English in saying *vind* and *varm* instead of *wind* and *worm.* § 154.

c. Supposing the Romans to possess English *v,* and the power of English *w* to be doubtful, the force of this argument may be tested by paraphrasing it for a Roman grammarian in this manner: "The English ear is certainly too delicate to suffer the pronunciation *worm* instead of *verm* (from VERMIS). We know, moreover, that in French the power of the characters *w* and *v* is identical, and that in German (whence the English probably borrowed it) the character *w* does not represent the semi-vowel contended for in English, so that the verb *went* was probably identical in sound with the noun *vent.*"

d. When an unusual sound, or a sound used in a mode to which we have not been accustomed, offends our prejudices, we are apt to persuade ourselves that our taste alone has been offended.

e. If English *w* is less pleasant than English *v,* *r* must be less pleasant than English *z,* the relation being about the same (§ 220); and whilst it accounts for the two English forms *hurrah* and *huzza,* it shows that to prefer the former is like preferring *wine* to *vine;* whilst to prefer the latter is like preferring *vine* to *wine.*

163. The proper character for English *v* in the Roman alphabet would be that of F with the middle line crossing the stem, so as to form a *Carvilium.* § 247.

165. ꓘ appears in the following inscription, from Manutius:—

$$\text{O C T A ꓱ I A E}$$
$$\text{C L A V D I I}$$
$$\text{C A I S A R I S}$$
$$\text{A V G V S T I . P . P}$$
$$\text{F I L I A E}$$

185*a.* "With regard to the Greek φ, there can be no doubt that it was a distinct p'h, like the middle sound in hap-hazard."—

Donaldson. There is no evidence that Mr. Donaldson was acquainted with the aspirate form of P.

b. An element cannot properly take its name from that which follows it, an error which is often committed in speaking of the Sanscrit post-aspirates like *th* in *foothold.*

187. "F PRO P ET ASPIRATIONE ACCIPITUR."—*Priscian.*

190*a.* "IMUM SUPERIS DENTIBUS APPRIMENS LABELLUM."—*Terentianus.*

b. The interchange between HIRCUS and FIRCUS, and his view that "no labial can pass to a guttural," have led Mr. Donaldson to adopt the theory that "The Latin F contained some guttural element, in addition to the labial of which it was in part composed... It seems to me that F must have been SV, or, ultimately, HV, and that V must have corresponded to our English w." Such a theory is unnecessary, because, according to Mr. Hale (see *Am. J. Sci.*, May, 1846, p. 319), the change from F and S, to H, is a peculiarity of the Hawaiian and Tahitian languages, when compared with the Polynesian standard. F is, in fact, composed of H pressed through the labio-dental contact, and if this is broken, the aspiration remains, which accounts for the change.

c. The same author adduces the Gothic *hv* and English *wh*, and the Greek and Latin mode of writing *rh*, as examples of transposition, but incorrectly, because the two modes represent an identical sound, like the old English [*hwen*] and English [*when*]. See note 224*d.*

197. According to Priscian, there were three varieties of L, *slender* (EXILE) as in ILLE; *full* (PLENUM) at the end of a syllable, or when preceding another consonant, as in SILVA, FLAVUS; and *ordinary* (MEDIUM) in other places, as in LECTUS; but we are not able to refer these to the various modern varieties of this letter, as the Welsh, Polish, or Hindu. One distinction must be made, that of doubling the sound where the character is doubled, as in *soulless.* § 19.

203. Gibbon ("Roman Empire," chap. 37) states, without authority, that the sounds of English *th* and *w* were unknown to the Greeks and Romans.

211. In Greek, when PₑNTₑ or PₑNT' *five*, and HEMI *semi* are united, the T and H are united into (ϑ) Th; and K followed by an aspirate becomes (χ) chi, as in DₑKA or DₑK', and HAMMA, which form DₑχAMMA, not DₑK'HAMMA (δεχάμμα), as if the post-aspirates were to be avoided. Some may think that this favors the post-aspirate view, although it is contradicted by comparing forms like DₑKA *ten*, and HₑX *six*, with DₑKAₑX *sixteen*, from which the aspirate is rejected. But in the Bengali, in which post-aspirates are common, H after P, as in P'HELA *fruit*, is often turned into F, forming FELA, although F is not otherwise a sound in this language. So the English name *Bent'ham* has become *Benth'am*.

213. The purely English notation [*sh*] (and its cognate [*zh*] used in the alphabet of Mr. Pickering) is not in consonance with the Latin alphabet, nor is it philosophical, [*s*] being already the representative of an aspirate, without the addition of [*h*]; so that in a Latin word [*sh*] would be read as in *mishap*.

223*a*. "Why does the third conjugation never receive the **z** in the future? *Ans.* Because every barytone future has the Σ, either actually or virtually, immediately before the Ω, as νοήσω, γράψω, λέξω: for the Ψ is composed of Π and Σ, and the Ξ of K and Σ; but as the **z** is composed, not of Δ and Σ, but of Σ and Δ, the future could not have the **z**, lest the Δ should virtually (δυνάμει) be found immediately before the Ω." This passage is particularly valuable, because it cannot have been corrupted to suit the views of transcribers after **z** had become *dz* in the modern languages.

b. The confusion caused by transcribers is shown in the case of the evidence of Verrius Flaccus respecting **z**. Thus the author of "Living Latin," p. 42, quotes him as saying of **z** that "SINE DUBIO MUTA FINIATUR;" whilst according to Schneider his words are "UT SINE MUTA FINIATUR."

c. The Greek **z** replaces the Hebrew ז zajin (as in זָרַ‎ח ZARA, St. Matt. i. 3), which is referred to English **z** in three German, one French, and three English versions of the Hebrew alphabet in my possession. Prof. Beleké informs me that Ewald assigns ס׳ as its power.

224*a*. z has become English *dzh* in a few words, as *zealous;* ZINZ*i*bER *ginger;* a replacement which is found in Persian. In Sclavonic words originally Greek, it has been replaced by English *zi, shi, zhi,* and *tshi.*

b. Marius Victorinus (if correctly edited) would have [z] represented by [DS] when written with Latin letters (*Schn.* p. 377), and among the moderns, Eichhoff, Bopp, Rapp, Lipsius, Scheller, Schneider, and the Portroyal Grammar, give precedence to the D. This is partly justified by the Sanscrit parallels of Greek, that of Z*ε*SIS having English *dzh,* and that of MYZ*ọ* English *tsh.* But the parallel of DAIZ*ọ*N has cerebral s; the Sanscrit RAS to *ring,* corresponds to the Greek RH*ŏ*IZ*ŏ*S a *loud noise;* and STAC to *sting* gave rise to STIZ*ọ.* z seems also to represent the Hebrew צ (§ 214) in part, as in AZEChES, עעק, with a prefix.

c. The following extract from the Portroyal Latin Grammar contains the views of those who believe that z represents DS. "It had something of the D, but with a very soft pronunciation; Mezentius as if Medsentius, &c. Hence it is" [not necessarily] "that the Dorians changed this letter into SD ... not that the z was equivalent to ςδ ... but by reason of a kind of transposition or metáthesis; both Flaccus and Longus observing, that as the X began with a C, the z *ought to* begin with D; so that all the double letters end with s. Yet Erasmus and Ramus pretend the contrary, and Sextus Empiricus" [in the second century] "endeavors to prove against the torrent of" [modern] "grammarians, that z was as much equivalent to ςδ as to δς.... Be that as it may, the Eolians also changed the δ into z, as ζαβαλλειν for διαβαλλειν, to *calumniate,* from whence they took ζαβολος (for διαβολος *devil*), which we meet with in St. Cyprian and St. Hilary."

d. The transposition alluded to is sufficiently common, as between CS and SC in ɹιξος and VISCUS *mistletoe;* the English *ask* or *acs,* and the Anglo-saxon *axian;* between *Ale C'Sandretta* and *S'Canderoon;* the German *borst* and Dutch *brost;* the French *règne* (in which the guttural follows) and the Latin REGNUM; and perhaps the Welsh or Irish *tarv* (*a* in *fat, r* trilled, *v* as in English) and the Latin TAVRUS a *bull.* The Latin words ALEX-

7

ANDER and MARMOR (*marble*, §§ 160, 215) have taken the forms ALEKSNADR and MRAMOR in Russian.

e. The Italian *ds* is probably tolerably ancient, and being incompatible with the Greek *sd*, there may have been a tendency to replace the latter with the former; but this has nothing to do with the acknowledged power of Greek *z* (§ 19) in Greek words, and it occurs in no others. SD occurs in Italian, as in *sdegno* (SDENJO) *indignation*, in which s is pure.

225*a*. "When the Greek *z* more nearly approximates to the sound of σδ, either this is preserved in the Latin transcriptions, as in Mesdentius, Sdepherus, for Mezentius, Zephyrus, or the δ is assimilated to the σ."—*Donaldson's Varronianus*, p. 218.

b. Buttmann (Dr. Robinson's ed., Andover, 1839), whilst he assigns *ds* to *z*, admits that "in the earlier periods" it was *sd;* and Kühner admits it in certain adverbs, as ἀϑήναζε for ἀϑήναςδε.

230*a*. The view combated in the text, which is founded upon a peculiarity of *English*, appears in *Donaldson's Varronianus*, where it is asserted that "the dental and guttural, when combined with [English] *y*, ... converge in the sound of our *j* or *sh*." That is, the Latin DJ might become *dzh*, although this would be as unlikely as the same change in German or Spanish.

b. The Latin J does not lengthen syllables by position, nor do the ancient grammarians enumerate it among the "double letters."

235. Martial uses the word IOTA as in English, for something very small; and the English *jot* is the same word corrupted by misunderstanding the initial letter, which is the *smallest* in the Hebrew alphabet. By perverting the character [J] and [O], the word *jot* has become perverted from *yote*. There is, however, nothing to prevent any one from going anew to the Latin for the correct word; since Dr. Johnson set the example of corrupting his vernacular by introducing a host of words believed to be Latin, instead of going to the living languages and dialects most nearly allied to English.

242*a*. "NQN INTER M ET N MEDIUM SONAT UNQVAM NONNUNQVAM ET SIMILIA, SED INTER N ET G."—*Marius Victorinus.* .

b. "INTER LITTERAS N ET G EST ALIA VIS, UT IN NOMINE

ANGVIS ET ANGARI ET ANCORAE ET INCREPAT ET
INCURRIT ET INGENUUS—IN OMNIBUS ENIM HIS NON
VERUM N, SED ADULTERINUM PONITUR."—*Nigidius Figulus,*
Schneider, i. 316. Had [G] represented a palatal sound in
INGENUUS and LONGINUS, the N would necessarily have remained
pure. § 268.

c. In Edwards and Taylor's translation (as it purports to be)
of Kühner's Greek Grammar, the correct term *guttural* is replaced
by *palatal,* although it is admitted of γ, x, χ, that "the *Germans*
pronounce these letters from the throat." It is something new
to have the *same* consonant formed at a *different* place by different
nations, as if there could be a palatal *b* or a guttural *t.* Nevertheless, if the view which these literary gentlemen take of [ʃγ]
is correct, the first of two gamma characters *does* represent a
palatal, namely, that of the English [*dzh*] in *judge,* because they
say that "γ before the palatals γ, x, χ, ξ . . . is sounded like *ng*
in *angel,*" which is neither the sound in *angle,* nor in *hanger,*
but that in *range,* so that the first gamma represents *dzh,* turning
ἄʃγελος into *a-dzh-γελος,* and λάϱυʃξ, not into the Latin LARYNX,
but into the French sounds *larunndjcs.* In the same work to ει
the power of *ei* (in rec*ei*ve? h*ei*ght? w*ei*ght?) is assigned, to ηυ
that of *ou* in *you* (correctly assigned to ου by Dr. Robinson), and
to ᴤ that which belongs to αυ, and this is converted into the vowel
in *laud.* If this is an honest translation, it is difficult to conceive
why Kühner should not know a vowel from a dipthong, or adduce
as a dipthong a vocal effect which is neither a vowel nor a dipthong.
Similar errors disfigure the Latin Grammar of Andrews and
Stoddard.

270. "K PENITUS SUPERVACUA EST."—*Priscian.* "K QVAE
NONNULLIS SUPERFLUA VIDETUR."—*Sergius.* "K LITTERA NON
SCRIBITUR NISI ANTE A."—*Probus.* (See *note* 290.)

276. "CUM DICO OBTINUIT . . . AVRES MAGIS AVDIUNT P."—
Quinctilian.

283. [LACRIMA] is found in the Carpensian manuscript of
Virgil. The inscriptive forms are taken from Manutius, who,
although he does not cite a single one with [Y], recommends the
word to be spelt with this character because it is so spelt in

Greek! It is probable that many similar barbarisms have been introduced into Latin orthography by officious copyists wedded to that useless minimum of etymology which may be preserved in a false orthography. The word in question was too common not to have become naturalized.

290. "K PERSPICUUM EST LITTERA QVOD VACARE POSSIT, ET Q SIMILIS, NAMQVE EADEM VIS IN UTRAQVE EST."—*Terentianus.* "Q... MULTI ILLAM EXCLUSERUNT, QVONIAM NIHIL ALIUD SIT QVAM C ET V, ET NON MINUS POSSIT SCRIBI QVIS PER C ET V ET I ET S."—*Vel. Long.* "QVIS QVIDAM PER CVIS SCRIBUNT, QVONIAM SUPERVACUAM ESSE Q LITTERAM PUTANT."—*Terent. Scaurus.* "NIGIDIUS FIGULUS IN COMMENTARIIS SUIS NEC K POSUIT PRO Q, NEC X."—*Marius Victorinus.* The proper reading seems to require NEC for PRO.

298. The use of [H] is somewhat irregular in the transcription of Biblical names, being correct in *Qedemah,* representing Ch in *Zohar,* and useless in *Abidah.* If it can properly replace Ch in *Zohar,* it might also be placed in *Phichol.*

The entomologist Fabricius correctly Latinized the German name *Hübner* into HYBNERUS, and *Cayenne* into CAJENNA; and some English naturalists properly represent the *w* of English names by the Latin character. In the following examples, the first column represents the *original,* the second an *incorrect,* and the third the *corrected* form of certain names, chiefly genera of plants:—

Banks	BANKSIA (note 270)	BANXIA.
Colebrooke	COLEBROOKIA (6 syllab.!)	COLBRUCIA.
Beatson	BEATSONIA (5 ")	BITSONIA.
Stewart	STEWARTIA	STJUARTIA.
Goodenough	GOODENOVIAE	GUDENOFIAE.
Wilkes	WILKESIA (note 270)	VILCSIA.
Büttner	BYTTNERIA	BYTNERIA.

ERRATA.

Page 45, end of line 12, for κλυστρη read κλυστης.

Page 48, line 13, for NG read NG.

Lightning Source UK Ltd.
Milton Keynes UK
UKOW01f0356050817
306737UK00005B/276/P